Student Workbook

Crisis Communications

A Casebook Approach

Second Edition

Student Workbook

Crisis Communications
A Casebook Approach

Second Edition

Kathleen Fearn-Banks
University of Washington

LEA
LAWRENCE ERLBAUM ASSOCIATES, PUBLISHERS
2002   **Mahwah, New Jersey**   **London**

Lawrence Erlbaum Associates, Inc., Publishers
10 Industrial Avenue
Mahwah, New Jersey 07430

Cover design by Kathryn Houghtaling-Lacey

ISBN 0-8058-3919-4 (alk. paper)

Printed in the United States of America

Contents

Preface

The Student Workbook is a supplement to the second edition of *Crisis Communications: A Casebook Approach.* It is primarily intended for use in crisis communications and public relations courses.

However, Chap. 2, "The Crisis Communications Plan," can be used by individuals and groups seeking to develop crisis communications plans (CCPs) for businesses and organizations. The CCP is different from the crisis management plan (CMP). The CMP includes overall steps for coping with a crisis (including evacuation procedures, antidotes for poisons, etc.), whereas the CCP stipulates how an organization communicates with key publics—the news media, employees, customers, and so forth—during a crisis.

For each textbook chapter, this workbook lists the key words and terms that should be understood. The instructor may or may not discuss the terms, but students should seek the definitions on their own. The workbook also includes exercises, pertinent documents, and other illustrations intended to contribute to the discussion and understanding of Chaps. 1–21 of the textbook. A comprehensive list of useful Web sites appears in Chap. 22.

—*Kathleen Fearn-Banks*

The Nature of Crises

VOCABULARY

After reading the chapter, write the definitions of the following terms. Then go back and test your own knowledge:

crisis management _____

_____

_____

_____

crisis communications _____

_____

_____

_____

publics _____

_____

_____

_____

crisis detection _____

_____

_____

_____

crisis preparation _____

_____

_____

_____

crisis prevention _____

_____

_____

_____

crisis containment _____

_____

_____

_____

crisis recovery _____

_____

_____

_____

crisis learning _____

_____

_____

_____

prodromes _____

_____

_____

_____

public opinion _____

_____

_____

_____

Excellence Theory _____
_____
_____
_____

strategy _____
_____
_____
_____

stakeholders _____
_____
_____
_____

strategically managed public relations _____
_____
_____
_____

segmentation _____
_____
_____
_____

risk communications _____
_____
_____
_____

organizational ideology _____
_____
_____
_____

communications ideology _____
_____
_____
_____

EXERCISE

The student body is a key public of your university or college. Segment that public into 10 groups:

1. _____

2. _____

3. _____

4. _____

5. _____

6. _____

7. _____

8. _____

9. _____

10. _____

CHAPTER TWO

The Crisis Communications Plan

VOCABULARY

Write the definitions of the following terms without referring to your textbook or notes:

enabling publics _____

_____

_____

_____

functional publics _____

_____

_____

_____

normative publics _____

_____

_____

_____

diffused publics _____

_____

_____

_____

THE CRISIS COMMUNICATIONS PLAN

Following is a step-by-step procedure for developing a crisis communications plan (CCP). As examples of most steps, sections of the CCP for UDUB Burger Drive-In (a fictitious name for an actual establishment) are reproduced here from Appendix C of the textbook. The plan addresses crises related to *E. coli* and hepatitis A poisoning. Your CCP may be similar or different depending on the crisis you choose for your plan.

The first step is to determine, through a crisis inventory, the type of crisis that would be most damaging and most likely for the business. Although not necessarily a part of the CCP, the inventory is a necessary step before developing a crisis plan.

Following the crisis inventory are the steps in the plan, and other examples from the UDUB Burger CCP. Names and other personal information from the real drive-in are omitted in the examples. However, the format of the charts and other CCP documents can be used by most organizations.

CRISIS INVENTORY

To determine an organization's most likely crises, the public relations department, with key executives, must take an inventory. A sample graph showing how crises are plotted and a blank graph for you to plot your own plan are provided in Figs. 2.1 and 2.2, respectively. Each possible crisis must be ranked as follows:

0—Impossible; that is, the crisis has basically no chance of occurring.

1—Nearly impossible.

2—Remotely possible.

3—Possible.

4—More than possible, somewhat probable; has happened to competitors or similar companies.

5—Highly probable; may or may not have previously occurred in company, but warning signs are evident.

Each crisis also should be ranked according to its potential damage to the company. The rankings in this category are as follows:

0—No damage; not a serious consequence.

1—Little damage; can be handled without much difficulty, not serious enough for the media's concern.

2—Some damage; a slight chance that the media will be involved.

3—Considerable damage; but still will not be a major media issue.

4—Considerable damage; would definitely be a major media issue.

5—Devastating; front-page news, could put company out of business.

For added security, when in doubt, rank a crisis in the next highest category.

For instance, Company Z may identify five crises that it could face: workplace violence, fire, protest demonstrations, negative legislation, and tax problems. Each might be ranked as shown in Table 2.1.

After rankings for probability and damage are made, bar graphs should be made to clearly show each crisis so that it can be compared to others. (Bar graphing can be done on various computer programs or by hand.) At the base of a blank graph, write the name of each type of crisis (see Fig. 2.1). Plot the height of each bar according to numbers attributed to each crisis in the probability and damage rankings. Choose different colors or shadings for probability bars and damage bars.

When Company Z plots its data on a bar graph, it resembles Fig. 2.1. Considering Company Z's graph, we see that the probability and seriousness of a crisis relating to tax problems is not as crucial as the other crises. Negative legislation, although a very likely crisis, seems not to be particularly critical. On the other hand, protest demonstrations are critical, although not very likely.

Workplace violence and fire seem both likely and critical.

TABLE 2.1
Company Z's Ranking of Crisis Probability and Damage

Crisis Type	Probability	Damage
Workplace violence	4	5
Fire	3	4
Protest demonstrations	2	5
Negative legislation	5	2
Tax problems	2	3

Company Z s Crisis Inventory

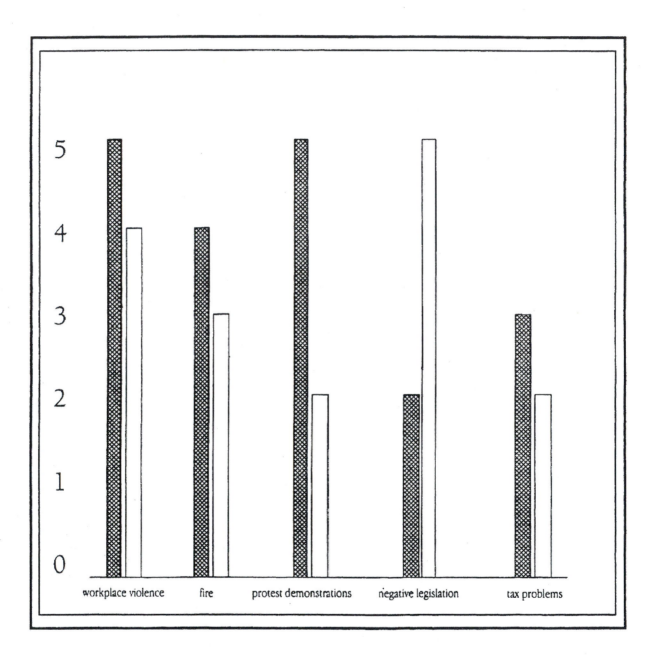

FIG. 2.1   A completed sample graph of a crisis inventory.

Crisis Inventory

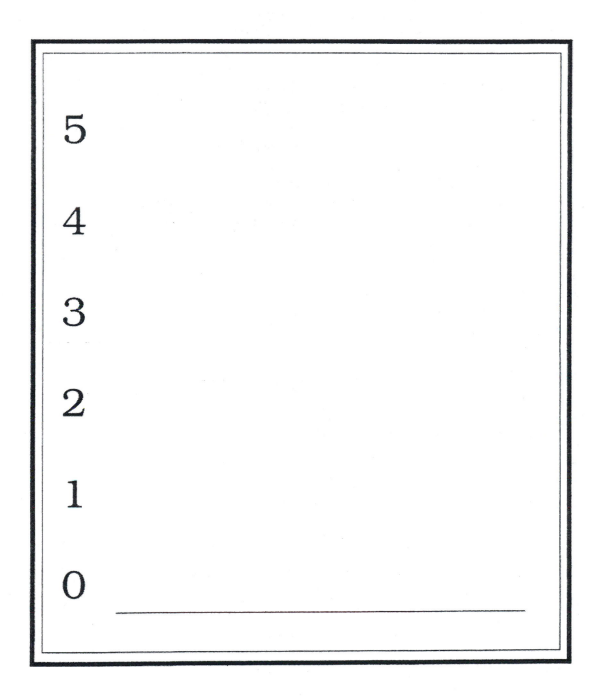

= damage   = probability

FIG. 2.2.   A blank graph for plotting a crisis inventory.

Most organizations plan for crises ranked high in both probability and damage. In this case, Company Z would probably develop crisis management and communications plans for workplace violence first, then for the other crises in descending order of importance: fire, protest demonstrations, negative legislation, and tax problems.

Sometimes, organizations make crisis plans for the most devastating crises, no matter how probable or improbable they may be. In this case, Company Z would develop plans for workplace violence first, followed by protest demonstrations, then fire.

The importance of the crisis inventory is to force organizations to think about the possibilities. The ranking procedure may introduce ideas for prevention programs. You also may realize that your organization is more vulnerable than you anticipated.

Crisis Inventory and Results

The accompanying crisis inventory graph (see Fig. 2.3) analyzes five possible crises that could occur at a UDUB Burger Drive-In: *E. coli* poisoning, hepatitis A poisoning, fire, injury, and violence. A study the probability of each possible crisis and the amount of possible damage that could result if that crisis occurred determined that UDUB Burger Drive-In is most vulnerable to the crisis involving *E. coli* and hepatitis A outbreaks. Hence, a crisis plan was created to suit the needs of UDUB Burger Drive-In in case one of these emergencies should occur.

ACTIVITY: DEVELOPING THE CRISIS COMMUNICATIONS PLAN

In case you plan to develop a CCP as a class project or as an independent project, the following pages take you step-by-step through the process. If you do not plan to do a CCP, turn to the exercise at the end of this chapter.

Before you draft a plan, you must first determine what crisis or crises the plan is intended to manage. You may develop one plan for various crises in which only certain pages will be different, or you may have different plans for different crises.

This activity is designed for one crisis. In order to use this section of the workbook effectively, it is suggested that a potential crisis be selected and followed throughout; for example, a hurricane, a flood, a fire, or food poisoning in the dorms. The crisis selected will make a difference in the compiling of lists and, of course, in the drafting of messages.

Step 1: Design the Cover Page

Write the title for the crisis communications plan; for example, "Crisis Communications Plan for Campus Violence at _____." Include the following:

The names of the person(s) writing the plan.

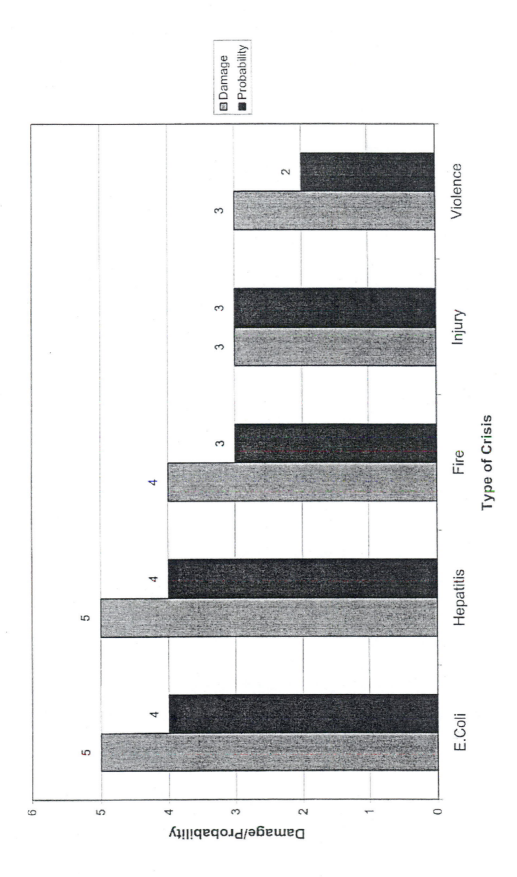

FIG. 2.3. Crisis Inventory Graph for UDUB Burger.

The date when the plan was written.
The dates when the plan was tested.

Write a draft of the cover page. An example follows:

UDUB Burger Drive-In's Crisis Communications Plan for *E. coli* and Hepatitis A
Crisis Communications Plan Team
School of Communications
University of Washington
Professor Kathleen Fearn-Banks

Written March 10, 1999

Dana Anderson
Jennifer Boyeson
Sarah Doran
Meg Hemphill
Stacy Jaffe
Melissa Jones
Jaime Kennerud
David Masin
Alexandra Ootkin
Danielle Rosenow
Julie Sanders
Diva Sze

Revised May 25, 1999

Sarah Doran
Meg Hemphill
Melissa Jones
Jaime Kennerud
Danielle Rosenow

Tested:

_____.

_____

_____

Step 2: Write the Introduction

Ask the head of the company to write answers to the following questions (or ask a PR professional to ghostwrite the answers):

Why is this plan important?

What can happen if it is not followed?

Have there been warning signs?

Has the crisis happened before here?

Has it happened to similar organizations?

The message should be persuasive and encouraging.

A table of contents should precede the introduction and acknowledgments. Following is a sample CCP introduction.

Introduction: Statement From Management to Employees

There are many high-risk factors surrounding the food industry, making it necessary for all food organizations to be ready for a potential crisis at any time. Our risks are heightened by the nature of our industry: We provide quick and simple food service. Especially with meat, there is a high risk of food poisoning if the meat is not cooked properly. Because of these dangers, it is vital that UDUB Burger's employees are prepared to deal with the media and the public quickly and efficiently in the event of a crisis.

We have worked for many years to build an impeccable reputation with the public by providing clean, quick, and quality service and food to our consumers. Because the most damaging scare in the food industry, particularly with hamburgers, is food poisoning—particularly the *E. coli* virus and hepatitis A—it is crucial that UDUB Burger be prepared for any possible circumstances involving a patron of our restaurant becoming ill from our food. The *E. coli* crisis that struck Jack-in-the-Box was a warning sign to all fast-food handlers. In order to prevent similar damage to our company, we must take very seriously what happened at Jack-in-the-Box and what Foodmaker did wrong in communicating with the media and the public.

If this CCP is not followed in the event of a crisis, irreparable damage to the reputation of UDUB Burger Drive-In is possible. The loss of trust among our consumers could also lead to a large loss of business. In dealing with this crisis plan, we must keep in mind that trust and reliability are incredibly important to consumers when choosing a place to eat, and UDUB Burger must protect its reputation as being a reliable fast-food source. We trust that you will all keep up the outstanding work in order to protect our company from such a crisis.

Step 3: Prepare Acknowledgments

Have key executives and key personnel in the plan sign this affidavit, verifying that they have read the plan and are prepared to put it into effect:

Acknowledgments

By signing this statement, I verify that I have read this CCP and am prepared to put it into effect.

Dick XXXX, President and CEO

_____
(Signature and date)

Jim XXXX, Vice President and CFO

_____
(Signature and date)

Walt XXXX, Vice President

_____
(Signature and date)

Jeanne XXXX, Office Manager

_____
(Signature and date)

Step 4: Schedule Rehearsal Dates

List the dates when the crisis plan was rehearsed (at least once or twice each year). Example:

Rehearsal Dates
June 24, 2001
August, 12, 2001

Step 5: State the Purpose and Objectives of the Plan

Keeping a specific crisis in mind, state the purpose and objectives of the plan, including the company's overall policy of communications. Following is an example from the UDUB Burger CCP.

Purpose

In the event of an *E. coli* or hepatitis A outbreak, we must take immediate action to inform our publics of the situation and the measures they need to take. Our open and honest transfer of information to the media and health care facilities will eliminate confusion among our publics. If we are truthful and forthright, the crisis situation can be more smoothly resolved and action can be taken to eliminate any future problems.

Objectives

In the event of a suspected *E. coli* or hepatitis A infection from food eaten at one of our restaurants, we will make every effort to:

1. Initiate the CCP within 2 hours.
2. Inform all health care organizations that might be involved with the situation.
3. Inform all owners and managers within 3 hours of the outbreak.
4. Inform the media and restaurant patrons within 4 hours of the outbreak.
5. Keep the media and all publics regularly informed of updated information.
6. Maintain honesty with the media about all known information.
7. Find the source of the problem as soon as possible.
8. Distribute our findings to the media and all publics.

9. Develop ways to alleviate future problems.
10. Implement necessary changes as soon as possible and resume business as usual.

Step 6: List Key Publics

In a format most convenient to the organization, list all key publics—both external and internal. You should probably rank them in order from most important to least important. The list should be comprehensive, including all publics and stakeholders with whom the organization must communicate during the crisis. Not every public needs to be notified in each crisis, but the list should be comprehensive. Unneeded publics can be eliminated at the time of the crisis.

All methods of reaching these stakeholders should be listed: office phone, home phone, car and cell phone, e-mail, neighbors, parents, vacation homes, clubs, and so on.

Notice the checklist for various media on pages 40, 41, and 42 (Figs. 2.8–2.10). Your list may take this form. You may decide to compile several lists, such as a city government list, a county government list, a state list, and a federal list. Maybe few or none of these apply to your organization. Develop the lists that are pertinent to you. Remember that if there are serious injuries or damages, officials not normally concerned with your organization will be very much concerned.

The following five charts list key publics and include information on how to notify them of crucial information.

List of Publics: Internal Key

In the event of a crisis, the following people should be informed immediately. A telephone tree should be used. The person who learns about the crisis first notifies Jim XXXX, vice president. Jim XXXX, then informs the Corporate General Partner and Operations Management groups. Ken XXXX, general manager, notifies the Restaurant Operations Group. The store managers then notify their employees. Lisa XXXX, director of training, notifies the Other Managers Group. These managers then notify their employees.

Name	Address	Office Phone	Cell Phone	Emergency Phone	Fax	E-mail
Corporate General Partner Group						
Dick XXXX, president and co-founder						
Ina Lou XXXX, executive vice president						
Jim XXXX, vice president and legal counsel						
Walt XXXX, vice president						
John XXXX, director of technical support						
Operations Management Group						
Ken XXXX, general manager						
Lisa XXXX, director of training						
Restaurant Operations Group						
Kim XXXX, 45th Street store manager						
Bert XXXX, Broadway store manager						
Jerry XXXX, Broadway substitute store manager						
Angie XXXX, Holman Road store manager						
Paul XXXX, Queen Anne store manager						
Other Manager Group						
Jeanne XXXX, office manager						
Jodie XXXX, training manager						
John XXXX, facilities/reserve manager						
Mel XXXX, facilities/projects manager						

Local Television News Personnel

Station/Channel	Address	News Director	Phone	Fax
KCTS/9	401 Mercer St. Seattle, WA 98109	Jane Sheridan	206-XXX-XXXX	206-XXX-XXXX
KING/5	333 Dexter Ave. N. Seattle, WA 98109	Eric Lerner Ron Taylor (weekend)	206-XXX-XXXX Newsphone: 206-XXX-XXXX	N/A
KIRO/7	2807 3rd Ave. Seattle, WA 98121	Bill Lord Tim Smith (assignment editor)	206-XXX-XXXX 206-XXX-XXXX Newsphone: 206-XXX-XXXX	206-XXX-XXXX
KOMO/4	100 4th Ave. Seattle, WA 98121	Joe Barnes Paula Marimon (weekend)	206-XXX-XXXX 206-XXX-XXXX	206-XXX-XXXX
KSTW/11	P.O. Box 141 Seattle, WA 98411	Dan Ackler Keith Groteluchen (weekend editor)	206-XXX-XXXX 206-XXX-XXXX	206-XXX-XXXX
KCPQ/13	1813 Westlake Ave. N. Seattle, WA 98109	Todd Mokhtari Cory Bertman (managing editor)	206-XXX-XXXX	N/A

Local Radio News Personnel

Station	Address	News Director	Phone	Fax
KING/1090 AM	333 Dexter Ave. N. Seattle, WA 98109	Tony Miner	206-XXX-XXXX	N/A
KIRO/710 AM	2807 3rd Ave. Seattle, WA 98121	Gail Neubert	206-XXX-XXXX	206-XXX-XXXX
KPLU/88 FM	121 St. & Park Tacoma, WA 98447	Michael Marcotte	206-XXX-XXXX	N/A
KUOW/94 FM	Univ. of WA Seattle, WA 98195	Marcie Stillman	206-XXX-XXXX	N/A
KOMO/1000 AM	100 4th Ave. Seattle, WA	Jennifer Beschel	206-XXX-XXXX	N/A

Local Newspaper Personnel

Newspaper	Address	Phone/Fax	When/Frequency
Seattle Post-Intelligencer City Editor: Kathy Best	101 Elliot Ave. W. Seattle, WA 98111	206-XXX-XXXX Fax: 206-XXX-XXXX	a.m. daily
Seattle Times City Editor: Bill Ristow	P.O. Box 70 Seattle, WA 98111	206-XXX-XXXX 260-XXX-XXXX	p.m. daily
Morning News Editor: Tom Osborne	P.O. Box 1100 Tacoma, WA 98411	253-XXX-XXXX	a.m. daily
Everett Herald Editor: Sam Strick	P.O. Box 930 Everett, WA 98206	425-XXX-XXXX	p.m. daily
Eastside Journal	1705 132nd Ave. NE Bellevue, WA 98005	206-XXX-XXXX Fax: 425-XXX-XXXX	p.m. daily
Eastside Week Editor: Pricilla Turner	123 Lake St. Kirkland, WA 98035	425-XXX-XXXX Fax: 425-XXX-XXXX	a.m. weekly
Seattle Weekly Editor: Knute Berger	1008 Western Ave. Suite 300 Seattle, WA 98104	206-XXX-XXXX Fax: 206-XXX-XXXX	a.m. weekly

Local Newswire Personnel

Name	Address	Editor	Phone	Fax
Associated Press News and Photo Bureau	201 Boren Ave. N., Room 5 Seattle, WA 98109	John Marlow	206-XXX-XXXX	206-XXX-XXXX
PR Newswire	1001 4th Ave., Suite 2138 Seattle, WA 98154	Derek Farley (bureau manager)	206-XXX-XXXX 800-XXX-XXXX	206-XXX-XXXX

Step 7: Identify the Crisis Team and Draft a Crisis Directory

Many organizations choose to place the crisis team directory near the beginning of the PLAN—after the cover page, introduction, and acknowledgments. Others feel that the crisis team, if rehearsed, knows its members, making this list less urgent than the list of key publics.

Regardless of where the directory appears, it should include all contact numbers, maybe even for neighbors, relatives, weekend homes, and so on. There should also be backups for each person.

This section should also identify the spokesperson and provide tips for him or her.

See Fig. 2.4 for an example of a crisis communications team directory. Write in the names that fit your organization.

Crisis Communications Team

TITLE	EMPLOYEE	OFFICE PHONE	CELL OR CAR PHONE	EMERGENCY PHONE	E-MAIL
Crisis Communications Manager *Duties:*					
Backup Crisis Communications Manager *Duties:*					
Assistant Crisis Communications Manager *Duties:*					
Crisis Control Room Coordinator *Duties:*					
Spokesperson 1 *Duties:*					
Spokesperson 2 *Duties:*					
Expert *Duties:*					
Print Media Contact Person 1 *Duties:*					
Print Media Contact Person 2 *Duties:*					
TV/Radio Media Contact Person *Duties:*					
Legal Advisor *Duties:*					

FIG. 2.4.   A sample crisis communications team directory.

Step 8: Identifying the Media Spokesperson

The Media Spokesperson

The media spokesperson represents the company and speaks on behalf of the company. The spokesperson must be selected very carefully. In addition, two or three backup spokespersons should be selected in advance in case the primary spokesperson is unavailable at the time of a crisis

Criteria for Selecting

- He/She must be powerful enough to make decisions and accessible throughout the crisis.
- He/She must be articulate, able to talk clearly, concisely, and in a pleasant manner.
- He/She must appear rational, concerned, and empathetic during a crisis.
- If more than one spokesperson is used, each one must all say the same thing.

Primary and Backup Spokespersons

	Office Phone	Cell Phone	Home Phone	E-mail
Spokesperson 1:	_____	_____	_____	_____
Spokesperson 2:	_____	_____	_____	_____
Spokesperson 3:	_____	_____	_____	_____
Spokesperson 4:	_____	_____	_____	_____

Interview Tips

- Prepare for answering *who, what, when, where, why,* and *how* questions.
- Focus on two or three key messages to communicate and repeat them during the interview.
- Gather background information that may be useful during the interview.
- Be aware of subjects, issues, and questions that might be brought up.
- Be accessible and pleasant to reporters. Show respect, and remember their names, if possible.

- Avoid saying, "No comment."
- Be honest.
- Remain calm, courteous, truthful, concerned, and, if necessary, apologetic.
- Face the reporter, not the camera or microphone.
- Avoid jargon. Speak in everyday language.
- Do not speculate. Do not answer questions you don't understand. Ask for clarification.
- Be trained ahead of time, rehearsed well in advance of the crisis, and briefed prior to responding to the media.

Trick Questions

Reporters might bring you into a difficult situation by asking you trick questions. Following are examples of various types of trick questions:

1. Speculative questions that begin with *if*:
   - "If the hamburgers that were infected were served during the normal lunch hour instead of late at night, how many people would have been infected?"
   - "If the hamburger had cooked at a higher temperature, would the *E. coli* outbreak have happened?"
2. Leading questions:
   "'You do agree that UDUB Burger could have avoided this crisis, right?"
3. Loaded questions:
   - "Isn't it true that you knew there was an *E. coli* outbreak but couldn't do anything to stop it at once, so it caused so many deaths?"
   - "Isn't it true that you knew of possible *E. coli* in the undercooked hamburgers?"
   - "Isn't it true that you knew this employee had hepatitis A and that you failed to do anything about it?"
   - Isn't it true that the shift manager should have been aware of the warning signs of this crisis?"
4. Naïve questions:
   - "What type of food does UDUB Burger Drive-In serve?"
5. False questions (containing inaccurate details that reporters want you to correct:
   - "There were only two employees during the rush hours, right?"

- "About 90% of your meat comes from the same plant that the contaminated meat from Jack-in-the-Box came from, correct?"
- "More than seven people have been affected by the virus strain that started here at your restaurant, right?"

6. Know-it-all questions:
   - "We have all the facts. I just need to confirm a few things with you, okay?"
   - "I have all of the details, but could you give me some wrap-up comment about this crisis?"

7. Silence: This tactic aims to get you to "spill your guts."

8. Accusatory questions (designed to make you blame someone else):
   - "Who is actually responsible for this crisis?"

9. Multiple-part questions (designed to be intentionally confusing):
   - "What is the temperature at which you cook your meat, and is that the regulation for Washington? If it is, then how can someone contract this virus if heat is supposed to kill it?"

10. Jargon questions: Make sure to avoid using technical words that can confuse publics no matter how the reporter phrases the question. It is usually easier to use the terms you use in the course of your profession, but they are not always understandable to outsiders.

11. Chummy questions:
    - "Hey, pal, off the record, why do you think this happened?"

12. Labeling questions:
    - "Would you say that the atmosphere here at UDUB Burger is 'stressful?'"
    - "Would you call the fast-paced environment stressful enough for one to lose sight of a specified task?"

13. Good-bye questions (reporters give the impression that the interview is over before asking such questions):
    - "Good-bye. Oh, by the way, how did this crisis actually happen?"

Step 9: List Emergency Personnel

Emergency personnel are usually not notified by Public relations personnel. They are usually part of the organization's more comprehensive crisis management plan (CMP). Often, however, if there is no CMP, PR personnel should also plan to notify the emergency personnel. PR frequently needs emergency numbers to call for gathering information, researching damage in a crisis, and so forth.

Make charts like those for the crisis team (Fig 2.4 on page 21). Here is an example from UDUB Burger's CCP:

List of Emergency Personnel

Seattle Police Department
610 3d, Seattle, WA 98104
Media Relations: 206-XXX-XXXX
Fax: 206-XXX-XXXX

Virginia Mason
925 Seneca, Seattle, WA 98101
Communications: 206-XXX-XXXX
Fax: 206-XXX-XXXX

Fire Department
301 2d, Seattle, WA 98104
Dept. Info: 206-XXX-XXXX
Fax: 206-XXX-XXXX

UW Medical Center
1959 NE Pacific St.,Seattle, WA 98105
PR: 206-XXX-XXXX
Fax: 206-XXX-XXXX

Harbor View Medical Center
325 9th Ave. S.,Seattle, WA 98104
PR: 206-XXX-XXXX
Fax: 206-XXX-XXXX

Swedish Medical Center
PR: 206-XXX-XXXX
Fax: 206-XXX-XXXX

King County Department of Health
206-XXX-XXXX

Step 10: List Equipment and Supplies for the Crisis Control Room

Include in this list the person responsible for getting each item and from where. Also crucial is the site of the control room. Alternate sites are important.

During a crisis, an appointed person (usually the crisis control room coordinator) gathers supplies and materials and checks off each item on the crisis plan list.

_____	chairs
_____	desks
_____	computers or typewriters
	(perhaps manual typewriters in case power is a problem)
_____	bulletin boards
_____	flip charts
_____	computer printers
_____	telephones
_____	cell phones
_____	battery-powered televisions and radios
_____	one or two chalkboards
_____	maps of the plant or crisis area
_____	battery-powered flashlights and lamps
_____	police radio
_____	walkie-talkies
_____	company letterhead
_____	pens
_____	pencils
_____	telephone directories
_____	contact lists
_____	media directories
_____	press kits
_____	CMPs and CCPs
_____	street and highway maps
_____	food and beverages
_____	copying machine
_____	first-aid kits
_____	cameras and film

Step 11: Pregather Information

Prepare and gather various documents that may possibly be needed during a crisis. Keep identical sets of these documents in various locales to ensure availability. Among the possibilities are these:

_____ Safety precautions
_____ Safety records
_____ Backgrounders
_____ Executive biographies
_____ Annual reports
_____ Photos
_____ Maps of sites
_____ Location of officers
_____ Fact sheets
_____ Phone books
_____ Fill-in-the-blanks news release
_____ Internet sources

The following five documents are samples of pregathered information for UDUB Burger Drive-In: a fill-in-the-blanks news release, cooking procedures, *E. coli* fact sheet, glossary, and Internet sources. (Also included in the CCP but not shown here are a history of UDUB Burger and information on its community relations programs, employee relations programs, and so forth.)

Fill-in-the-Blanks News Release

Press Release

For Immediate Release
(Date)

A UDUB Burger Drive-In customer is being treated for (*illness*) at (*hospital*). (*His/Her*) condition is (_____ _____ _____ _____ _____).
As of right now it is unknown if (*he/she*) contracted (*illness*) at the (_____) UDUB Burger location, where (*he/she*) ate (*when*).

"We are very concerned about (*victim's name*), and we are monitoring (*his/her*) condition. Whether the illness came from food at UDUB Burger or some other source, we wish for (*his/her*) speedy recovery," UDUB President Dick XXXX said.

(*Victim's name*) ate (*what victim ate*) at the UDUB Burger Drive-In in (*location*). (*Victim's name*) became ill (*when*) after experiencing (*side effects/symptoms*).

Officials at UDUB Burger took immediate action to see if it is possible that the illness is a direct result of eating contaminated food at the restaurant. At this time, they have not found any evidence, but they are continuing their investigation.

There have been no reported cases of (*illness*) from eating at UDUB Burger in the restaurant's 45-year history.

UDUB Burger has a strict sanitary code that requires employees to cook hamburgers to 160 degrees, 10 degrees higher than required by the U.S. Food and Drug Administration (FDA). Employees are thoroughly trained in cooking, safety, and health procedures.

(*E. coli* is a bacterium that comes in many forms, most of which are harmless. Distinctive symptoms include abdominal cramps and bloody diarrhea. These symptoms appear 3 to 5 days after eating contaminated food and usually go away in 6 to 8 days. Symptoms of hepatitis A include fatigue, vomiting, jaundice, pain in the liver area, and dark urine. These symptoms can appear up to 50 days after ingesting contaminated food. There is currently no treatment for the disease, although rest and proper nutrition can relieve some symptoms.)

Cooking Procedures

- UDUB Burger cooks all hamburgers to 160 degrees, which is 10 degrees higher than required by the FDA.
- UDUB Burger uses temperature-taking procedures to ensure that the hamburgers are cooked to 160 degrees.
- All employees of UDUB Burger have a food-handler permit.
- Employees are trained in cooking, safety, and health procedures.

Employee safety and health information can be found in the *Employee Handbook*.

E. coli Fact Sheet

Definition of E. coli. *E. coli* is an emerging cause of food-borne illness. *E coli* are germs (bacteria) that normally live in the intestines of people and animals. There is no treatment for *E. coli*.

What Are the Symptoms? The most common symptoms are severe stomach cramps and diarrhea. Some people vomit or run a fever, but these symptoms are less common. These symptoms usually go away by themselves after 6 to 8 days. In a small number of people, this strain of *E. coli* can cause a rare but serious problem called hemolytic uremic syndrome (HUS).

What is HUS? HUS is a disease that affects the kidneys and blood-clotting system. In severe cases, dialysis is used for a limited time to do the kidney's work. Some people also develop a bleeding problem or low red blood-cell count (anemia).

Where Is E. coli Found? It lives in the intestines of healthy cattle and gets into the meat when cattle are slaughtered. The germs are killed when the meat is thoroughly cooked. Germs have also been found in raw milk, apple cider, and salami.

How Is E. coli Spread? *E coli* must be swallowed to cause an infection. This can happen if you eat or drink something that contains these germs and is not properly cooked or pasteurized. The germs can be spread from person to person if someone who is infected does not thoroughly wash his or her hands with soap and water before preparing food for others.

How Is E. coli Prevented? Take the following steps to avoid infection:
- Do not eat nonpasteurized dairy products or undercooked ground beef.
- Do not drink raw milk or apple cider that is made from unwashed apples.
- Always wash your hands with soap and water after going to the bathroom, changing a diaper, or handling raw meat.

Glossary of Food-Related Illnesses

Botulism: A disease caused by contamination of certain foods by the botulism bacterium commonly found in the soil. The botulism toxin is produced when the bacteria grow in improperly canned foods and occasionally in contaminated seafood. Common symptoms are headaches, nausea, vomiting, constipation, and overall weakness. It progressively attacks the nervous system, causing double vision, muscle paralysis, and difficulty with breathing and speech. Symptoms appear 8 to 12 hours after eating contaminated food. Death may occur within 3 to 7 days without treatment. There is an antitoxin to treat the disease.

Campylobacteriosis: Bacteria found in the intestinal tracts of healthy animals and untreated water surfaces. Inadequately cooked animal products and nonchlorinated water are the most common reasons for human infection. It can be easily killed by heat above 120 degrees Fahrenheit. Common symptoms are abdominal cramping, diarrhea, fever, headache, muscle pain, and nausea. Symptoms appear 2 to 5 days after eating contaminated food and may last 2 to 7 days.

Clostridium Perfringens: Bacteria found in soil, unprocessed foods, nonpotable water, and the intestinal tract of humans and animals. It is a milder form of botulism. Symptoms include abdominal pain and diarrhea. Symptoms appear 8 to 24 hours after eating contaminated food and may last 1 to 2 days.

***E. coli* Hemolytic Colitis**: Bacteria that comes in many forms; most are harmless except the *E coli 0157:H7* strain. Abdominal cramps and bloody diarrhea are the distinctive symptoms of this strain. Other symptoms are fever, nausea, and vomiting. These symptoms appear 3 to 5 days after eating contaminated food. Symptoms may last 10 days.

Hepatitis A Virus: A highly contagious virus that attacks the liver. The virus is transmitted by the fecal–oral route, through close person-to-person contact or by ingesting contaminated food or water. Common symptoms are fatigue, nausea, vomiting, fever, jaundice, pain in the liver area, dark urine, and abdominal pain. The disease can stay in the body for 10 to 50 days without producing symptoms. Recovery usually takes 1 to 2 weeks.

Listeriosis: Bacteria that live in humans and animals. Listeriosis is usually associated with cattle and sheep having abortions and encephalitis. The elderly, newborn babies, pregnant women, and people with a weakened immune system are the most vulnerable to this infection. Possible symptoms are fever, headaches, nausea, and vomiting. Symptoms appear 3 days to a few weeks after eating contaminated food and may last several days. Death may occur in rare cases.

Salmonellosis: Bacteria spread through contact with human or animal intestinal contents or excrement, usually found in raw meat, fish, poultry, and eggs. Symptoms, which are headache, vomiting, nausea, chills, fever, diarrhea, and abdominal cramping, appear 12 to 36 hours after someone has eaten contaminated food. The symptoms may last 2 to 7 days.

Staphylococcal Intoxication: Bacteria found on the skin and in the nose and throat of most humans. People with sinus infections and colds are high-risk carriers. Infected wounds are rich sources of this bacterium. Sewage, raw milk, and untreated water are carriers. Symptoms include vomiting, nausea, diarrhea, and abdominal cramping. Symptoms appear 1 to 8 hours after eating contaminated food and may last 1 to 2 days.

INTERNET SOURCES

http://www.cdc.gov/ncidod/ncid.htm

National Center for Infectious Diseases (NCID) Web site

- Learn about the NCID
- Disease information
- Bacterial information
- Access *Emerging Infectious Diseases* journal

http://www.doh.wa.gov/Topics/ecoli.htm

Public Fact Sheet About *E. coli*

- What is it?
- Who gets it?
- How does it spread?
- What are the symptoms?
- How is it diagnosed?

http://www.doh.wa.gov/Topics/hepafact.html

Public Fact Sheet About Hepatitis A

- What is hepatitis A?
- How does it spread?
- How is it contracted?
- Overall history

http://www.jackinthebox.com

Jack-in-the-Box Web Site

http://ificinfo.health.org

International Food Information Council Web Site

http://www.odwalla.com

Odwalla Web Site

Step 12: Develop Key Messages

Messages must be tailored to each public, just as means of communication are selected for each public. The first statement made to each public sets the stage for the rest of the crisis. It establishes credibility or lack of it.

The statement to all publics should include information about the nature of the crisis, emergency, or accident; the 5 Ws and H (*what*, *where*, *when*, *why*, *who*, and *how*); the steps the organizations will take to recover; and a report on the deaths or injuries. It should also include a comment about the corporate culture revealing the corporate policy. This shows the company has a heart..

Key messages can be drafted in advance and altered at the time of the crisis to fit the occasion. Advance preparation allows the PR professional to organize the statement carefully without stress.

Key messages may change as the crisis develops. Examples of key messages are:

"At this company, safety is more important than production."
"Our employees are our first priority."

Once notification of the crisis have been made and initial key messages have been relayed, strategies designed to accomplish objectives are established. Then tactics are devised to fit the key messages, the public, and the strategy. All messages may be altered as the crisis develops.

Following are sample key messages about *E. coli* and hepatitis A from the UDUB Burger CCP.

Samples of Company Position and Key Messages

E. coli

In the event of an *E. coli* outbreak, UDUB Burger employees, first priority is the care of customers. Warning the public of the symptoms of *E. coli* is the first order of business. The symptoms can include one or more of the following: abdominal cramps, bloody diarrhea, and nausea. Our primary concern is with those who are infected with *E. coli*. Without knowing the exact location where the *E. coli* originated, whether from the meat distributor or inside our store, we promise the public that the source of the bacteria will be discovered as promptly and effectively as possible.

We will also restate consistently the fact that we are concerned with the *E. coli* problem and that our primary concern is for those infected. We will restate how careful and cautious UDUB Burger is in preventing diseases such as this one from occurring. We will state that our employees cook meat to the standard temperature set by the FDA and that employees follow proper cleaning procedures outlined by the FDA. We will explain that our employees are required to receive a food-handlers permit prior to working at UDUB Burger.

The following key messages should be stressed in the order indicated:

1. Our biggest concern is for those affected.
2. We are sorry for what happened and we take full responsibility for what happened.
3. We don't know how it happened, but we are trying to find out, and we'll let you know as soon as we know.
4. We maintain a strict and thorough process on avoiding problems such as these from occurring by requiring our employees to receive a food handler's permit.

Hepatitis A

In the event of a hepatitis A scare, UDUB Burger employees' first priority is the care of customers. Warning the public of the symptoms of hepatitis A is the first order of business. The symptoms can include one or more of the following: fatigue, nausea, vomiting, fever/chills, jaundice, pain in the liver area, dark urine, light-colored stools, and/or abdominal pain. Our primary concern is with those who are infected with hepatitis A. Without knowing the exact location where the hepatitis A originated, whether from one of the employees or an external source, we promise the public that the source of the disease will be discovered as promptly and effectively as possible.

We will also restate consistently the fact that we are concerned with the hepatitis A problem and that our primary concern is for those infected. We will restate how careful and cautious UDUB Burger is in preventing diseases such as this one from occurring. We will state that employees are required to receive a food-handler permit prior to working at UDUB Burger and that they must wash their hands before handling any food.

The following key messages should be stressed in the order indicated:

1. Our biggest concern is for those affected.
2. We are sorry for what happened and we take full responsibility for what happened.
3. We don't know how it happened, but we are trying to find out, and we'll let you know as soon as we know.
4. We maintain a strict and thorough process on avoiding problems such as these from occurring by requiring our employees to receive a food handler's permit.

Step 13: Plan Dissemination of Key Messages

Determine the best methods of communicating key messages to key publics, including the media. Also determine who on the crisis team will be responsible for the communication to each key public.

Checklists for each branch of the news media (Figs. 2.8–2.10) follow the overall plan for communications (Fig. 2.5). Figs. 2.7 through 2.10 are for your use.

YOUR COMPANY

MESSAGE: There has been an explosion in the plant. There are injured employees. We do not know, at this time, the cause of the explosion or the extent of injuries of the employees. An investigation is underway.

Methods of Communication

PUBLICS	TELEPHONE	E-MAIL	FAX	LETTER BY MESSENGER	LETTER BY MAIL	NEWSLETTER	BULLETIN BOARD	PERSONAL VISIT	NEWS RELEASE	MEETINGS
EMPLOYEES		* J. Naas				* J. Naas	* J. Naas			
EXECUTIVES	* Nelson J.	* Nelson J.						* Nelson J. / M. Yerima		* Nelson J.
CUSTOMERS					* Damian L.					
BOARD OF DIRECTORS	* Nelson J.			* Damian L.					* Gina A.	
ELECTRONIC MEDIA	* K. Stone		* K. Stone						* Gina A.	
DAILY NEWSPAPERS	* Gina A.		* Gina A.						* Gina A.	
WEEKLY NEWSPAPERS					* Damian L.					
SHARE HOLDERS		* Ann C.				* Ann C.				
COMMUNITY LEADERS			* Karen N.			* Karen N.				

* Staff member responsible for communications and followup.

FIG. 2.5. A sample chart showing key publics of a fictitious organization, methods of communications, and crisis personnel responsible for the communications. The key message is written at the top of the chart.

Your Company

Message:

Methods of Communication

	Telephone	Electronic Mail	Fax	Letter by Messenger	Letter by Mail	Newsletter	Bulletin Board	Personal Visit	News Release	Meetings
P										
U										
B										
L										
I										
C										
S										

FIG. 2.6. A blank chart for plotting an organization's publics, communications methods, personnel responsibilities, and key message.

Crisis Communications Checklist

Nature of Crisis _____

_____

Date of Occurrence _____ Time _____

Response	By Whom	Date	Time	Comments
Crisis center set up.				
Crisis team mobilized.				
Key stakeholders notified:				
CEO				
Lawyer				
Mayor				
Union officials				
Insurance agent				
_____				
_____				
Basic facts gathered.				
What happened?				
When?				
Cause?				
Number of deaths?				
Number of injuries?				
Extent of damage?				
Names/titles of deceased?				
Names/titles of injured?				
What is being done?				
Emergency officials at scene?				
Estimated return to normalcy?				

FIG. 2.7. A crisis communications checklist: When each activity is completed, the person, date, and time are recorded. Important comments are also included.

Response	By Whom	Date	Time	Comments
Notification of nearest of kin of deceased or injured?				
Dissemination of facts of crisis?				
Contact company officials				
Contact city officials				
Contact county officials				
Contact state officials				
Contact federal officials				
Contact employees				
Contact emergency officials				
Contact stockholders				
Contact board of directors				
Contact volunteers				
Contact neighbors				
Contact community leaders				
Contact competitors				
TV Station 1				
TV Station 2				
Radio News Station 1				
Radio News Station 2				
Newspaper 1				
Newspaper 2				
News Conference				

FIG. 2.7. (continued)

TELEVISION NEWS CHECKLIST

Station Call Letters	Channel	Address	News Director	Phone	Fax

FIG. 2.8.   A blank television news checklist for filling in the contact names and numbers for all the persons who may be needed at television news stations.

RADIO NEWS CHECKLIST

Station Call Letters	Dial #	Address	News Director	Phone	Fax

FIG. 2.9.   A blank radio news checklist for filling in the names and numbers of radio personnel needed in a crisis.

NEWSPAPER CHECKLIST

Name of Newspaper	Who Contacted?	When Contacted?	Response?	Circulation

FIG. 2.10. A blank newspaper checklist for filling in the names of newspaper editors, reporters, and others needed during a crisis.

Step 14: Review Draft of the Crisis Plan and Make Corrections

Step 15: Distribute Plan to All Members of the Crisis Team

Step 16: Review and Update the Plan Once Each Year

Step 17: Drill and Rehearse Plan

Step 18: Drill and Rehearse With Spokespersons

Step 19: Evaluate the Plan.

The following sample document is from UDUB Burger's crisis plan.

Evaluation of Plan Effectiveness After a Crisis

After a crisis, the following steps will be followed to ensure that UDUB Burger is better prepared for the future. This evaluation is for looking at what went right and what went wrong during the crisis. It covers all aspects of the crisis, including media relations, community relations, and the crisis management team's performance. It is vital to evaluate the company's CCP while the crisis is still fresh in employees' minds. Thinking about all aspects of the crisis will help determine what we can do better next time.

1. Media relations: Review the media's coverage of the crisis. Were there areas in which we could have received better or more positive coverage of our company? Would the coverage have been better if we had taken the time to build strong media relationships before the crisis?

2. Community relations: Did the community act favorably to how we handled the crisis? If not, what can we do to build better community relations (i.e., public service donations or activities)? If we donate money or services, make sure that the public is aware of it (through media coverage or information at our restaurant locations).

3. Crisis management team: Did all team members perform well under pressure? Were there certain members who should have been put "behind the scenes" or on the "front lines" (speaking to the media, etc.)? Should any members be replaced by others should another crisis occur? Was the crisis control room properly stocked? Was there anything missing that needs to be ordered or created?

EXERCISE

In Chapter 1, you segmented the student body public. Now make a list of enabling publics, functional publics, normative publics, and diffused publics of the college or university—persons who would be notified in the event of a particular crisis, such as an earthquake. Remember that all contact numbers are essential: home phone, office phone, fax, e-mail, car phone, and pager. For this example, however, office numbers will suffice.

Name	Address	Contact Number
_____	_____	_____
_____	_____	_____
_____	_____	_____
_____	_____	_____
_____	_____	_____
_____	_____	_____
_____	_____	_____
_____	_____	_____
_____	_____	_____
_____	_____	_____
_____	_____	_____
_____	_____	_____
_____	_____	_____
_____	_____	_____
_____	_____	_____

CHAPTER THREE

Crisis Makers

VOCABULARY

rumor _____

_____

_____

_____

intentional rumor _____

_____

_____

_____

premature-fact rumor _____

_____

_____

_____

malicious rumor _____

_____

_____

_____

outrageous rumor _____

_____

_____

_____

nearly true rumor _____

_____

_____

_____

birthday rumor _____

_____

_____

_____

"gotcha" journalism _____

_____

_____

_____

sensationalism _____

_____

_____

_____

newsmongering _____

_____

_____

_____

checkbook journalism _____

_____

_____

_____

non-expert expert _____

_____

_____

_____

EXERCISES

1. What rumors have you heard recently? Describe the rumors and how they were
    communicated to you? What made the rumors believable or not so believable? Did
    you repeat the rumors to others? Could any of the rumors damage the reputation
    of a person or organization? Write your answers here:

    _____

    _____

    _____

    _____

    _____

    _____

    _____

    _____

    _____

    _____

    _____

    _____

    _____

    _____

    _____

    _____

    _____

    _____

    _____

    _____

    _____

    _____

    _____

    _____

    _____

2. Think about what can be done to stop rumors. Write what you think might be an effective means of fighting false rumors. Cite specific types of rumors.

_____

_____

_____

_____

_____

_____

_____

_____

_____

_____

_____

_____

_____

_____

_____

_____

_____

_____

_____

_____

_____

_____

_____

_____

3. Watch TV news broadcasts or TV newsmagazine programs, looking for hidden-camera segments, and scrutinize segments of "gotcha" journalism. Consider whether the charges leveled against the targeted business or person may not be true. See if there is any possible defense that would convince you the subject is not guilty of the charge. Is the coverage fair? What did the hidden camera or reporter do that might be considered "over the line"?

_____

_____

_____

_____

_____

_____

_____

_____

_____

_____

_____

_____

_____

_____

_____

_____

_____

_____

_____

_____

_____

_____

4. Chapter 10, "Case: Cellular Phones and The Cancer Scare," is a story of a non-expert expert. What other non-expert experts have you seen on television or heard on radio? Why are they convincing? What can be done to stop the damage they do?

_____

_____

_____

_____

_____

_____

_____

_____

_____

_____

_____

_____

_____

_____

_____

_____

_____

_____

_____

_____

_____

_____

CHAPTER FOUR

Cyber Crises: Rogue Sites and E-mail Rumors

VOCABULARY

search engine _____

_____

_____

_____

domain names _____

_____

_____

_____

rogue Web site _____

_____

_____

_____

spoof sites _____

_____

_____

_____

Anticybersquatting Consumer Protection Act of 1999 _____

_____

_____

_____

federal trademark registration _____

_____

_____

_____

Network Solutions, Inc. (NSI) _____

_____

_____

_____

DISCUSSION AND ACTIVITIES

1. Check the Urban Legends Web site—urbanlegends.minigco.com—for Internet
    hoaxes and e-mail rumors. Be prepared to discuss. How damaging could the
    hoaxes and rumors be to companies, organizations, or individuals? How could the
    affected organizations or individuals fight effectively?

    _____

    _____

    _____

    _____

    _____

    _____

    _____

    _____

    _____

    _____

    _____

    _____

    _____

    _____

    _____

    _____

    _____

    _____

    _____

    _____

    _____

    _____

EXERCISES

1. Find a rogue Web site on the Internet, and describe your response to it. Write a response that could be printed in a newspaper, circulated via e-mail, or posted on a Web site. Which method of responding would be the most effective and why?

2. Search the Internet for other rogue Web sites. Consider why the sites were created any by whom (e.g., angry exemployees, disgruntled customers, etc.). Also search the Internet for organizations or companies attacked and how they defended themselves (e.g., check their Web sites for responses to the attack sites). What damage could be done to the organizations attacked? If you were hired by one of these companies or organizations to remedy the situation, what would you do?

_____

_____

_____

_____

_____

_____

_____

_____

_____

_____

_____

_____

_____

_____

_____

_____

_____

_____

DISCUSSION AND ACTIVITIES

Following are some comments by experts on the killer banana e-mail hoax. These quotes were reported on APBNews.com. Your instructor may use these quotes for class discussion.

a. Tim Debus, vice president of the International Banana Association (IBA): "The rumor is just another case of Internet terrorism like the recent hacker attacks on popular Web sites."

b. Centers for Disease Control (CDC) and Food and Drug Administration (FDA) advisory board: "FDA and CDC agree that the bacteria [necrotizing fasciitis] cannot survive long on the surface of a banana. The usual route of transmission for these bacteria is from person to person."

c. John Shieh, a consultant to the National Necrotizing Foundation: "The mere ingestion of these bacteria would only make you sick with vomiting and diarrhea. [Eating] will not cause you to get a necrotizing fasciitis. Don't worry about the bananas, anyway. Most of them you buy are from the USA."

d. Chiquita Brands International (CBI): "The report currently circulating on the Internet concerning Costa Rican bananas being contaminated with a rare bacteria is totally false. Chiquita has received no reports of such contamination, and we have checked with the pertinent U.S. government agencies, which also confirm no reports of such contamination."

Date: Thu, 24 Feb 2000   11:44:37 0500
From: XXXXX   < XXXX@cdc.gov >
To: K. Fearn-Banks
Subject: FW: "Banana Warning"

Kathleen,

This is a false report. Please go to the CDC homepage, "In the News," press releases. There is one dated Jan. 28 that addresses this.

http://www/cdc.gov/od/oc/meida/pressrel/r2ko128.htm

In a message dated 2/14/00 6:58:14 PM Pacific Standard Time, XXX writes:

Vital Information regarding contaminated bananas. Please forward to everyone you love! I have checked the source and it is VALIDATED FROM THE CDC (Center for Disease Control in Atlanta, Georgia).

Warning: Several shipments of bananas from Costa Rica have been infected with necrotizing fasciitis, otherwise known as flesh-eating bacteria. Recently this disease has decimated the monkey population in Costa Rica. We are now just learning that the disease has been able to graft itself to the skin of fruits in the region, most notably the banana, which is Costa Rica's largest export. Until this finding, scientists were not sure how the infection was transmitted.

It is advised not to purchase bananas for the next three weeks as this is the period of time for which bananas that have been shipped to the United States with the possibility of carrying this disease. If you have eaten bananas in the last 2-3 days and come down with a fever followed by a skin infection, seek medical attention.!!!

The skin infection from necrotizing fasciitis is very painful and eats two to three centimeters of flesh per hour. Amputation is likely; death is possible. If you are more than an hour from a medical center, burning the flesh ahead of the infected area is advised to help slow the spread of the infection.

The FDA has been reluctant to issue a countrywide warning because of fear of nationwide panic. They have secretly admitted that they feel upwards of 15,000 Americans will be affected by this, but that these are not acceptable numbers.

Please forward this to as many people you care about as possible.

FIG. 4.1. The killer banana e-mail hoax: This is a copy of the e-mail attack on the banana industry circulated in early 2000. Names of persons were eliminated. Note that the Center for Disease Control, which the letter said validated the "killer bananas," says the report is false. Like most e-mail hoaxes, this one cited a reliable source, like the CDC, and contained several clues indicating that the message was fabricated. What clues can you find in the letter? The hoaxters will never reveal their identity.

Date:
From: XXXX
To: Kathleen Fearn-Banks
Subject: Info

You won't believe what happened to me yesterday. I was on my way to the post office to pick up my case of free M&M's (sent to me because I forwarded an e-mail to five other people, celebrating the fact that the year 2000 is "MM" in Roman numerals), when I ran into a friend whose neighbor, a young man, was home recovering from having been served a rat in his bucket of Kentucky Fried Chicken (which is predictable, since as everyone knows, there's no actual chicken in Kentucky Fried Chicken, which is why the government made them change their name to KFC).

Anyway, one day this guy went to sleep and when he awoke he was in his bathtub and it was full of ice and he was sore all over and when he got out of the tub he realized that HIS KIDNEY HAD BEEN STOLEN. He saw a note on his mirror that said "Call 911!" but he was afraid to use his phone because it was connected to his computer, and there was a virus on his computer that would destroy his hard drive if he opened an e-mail entitled "Join the crew!" He knew it wasn't a hoax because he himself was a computer programmer who was working on software to prevent a global disaster in which all the computers get together and distribute the $250.00 Neiman-Marcus cookie recipe under the leadership of Bill Gates. (It's true—I read it all last week in a mass e-mail from BILL GATES HIMSELF, who was also promising me a free Disney World vacation and $5,000 if I would forward the e-mail to everyone I know.)

The poor man then tried to call 911 from a pay phone to report his missing kidney, but a voice on the line first asked him to press #90, which unwittingly gave the bandit full access to the phone line at the guy's expense. Then reaching into the coin return slot he got jabbed with an HIV-infected needle around which was wrapped a note that said, "Welcome to the world of AIDS."

Luckily he was only a few blocks from the hospital—the one where that little boy who is dying of cancer is, the one whose last wish is for everyone in the world to send him an e-mail and the American Cancer Society has agreed to pay him a nickel for every e-mail he receives. I sent him two e-mails and one of them was a bunch of X's and O's in the shape of an angel (if you get it and forward it to more than 10 people you will have good luck, but for 10 people only you will have OK luck, and if you send it to fewer than 10 people you will have BAD LUCK FOR SEVEN YEARS). So anyway the poor guy tried to drive himself to the hospital, but on the way he noticed another car driving without its lights on. To be helpful, he flashed his lights at him and was promptly shot as part of a gang initiation.

Send THIS to all the friends who send you their junk mail and you will receive 4 green M&M's. If you don't the owner of Proctor & Gamble will report you to his Satanist friends and you will have more bad luck: you will get sick from the Sodium Laureth Sulfate in your shampoo, your spouse/mate will develop a skin rash from using the antiperspirant which clogs the pores under your arms, and the U.S. government will put a tax on your e-mails forever.

I know this is all true 'cause I read it on the Internet and in e-mail.

FIG. 4.2. This widely circulated e-mail message. This e-mail letter, obviously intended as a joke, was circulated widely and taken seriously by numerous people who passed it on to friends hoping to warn them. (*Source*: ?????????)

UNITED STATES POSTAL SERVICE® *Postal News*

FOR IMMEDIATE RELEASE
May 21, 1999
Release No. 99-045

E-MAIL RUMOR COMPLETELY UNTRUE

WASHINGTON—A completely false rumor concerning the U.S. Postal Service is being circulated on Internet e-mail. As a matter of fact, the Postal Service has learned that a similar hoax occurred recently in Canada concerning Canada Post.

The e-mail message claims that a "Congressman Schnell" has introduced "Bill 602P" to allow the federal government to impose a 5-cent surcharge on each e-mail message delivered over the Internet. The money would be collected by Internet Service Providers and then turned over to the Postal Service.

No such proposed legislation exists. In fact, no "Congressman Schnell" exists.

The U.S. Postal Service has no authority to surcharge e-mail messages sent over the Internet, nor would it support such legislation.

###

FIG. 4.3. The U.S. Postal Service disseminated this news release on May 21, 1999, in an attempt to stop an unfounded e-mail rumor. (*Source*: U.S. Postal Service Web page: http://www.usps.com/news/email.htm. Reprinted by permission.)

CHAPTER FIVE

Managing a Crisis

VOCABULARY

puffery _____

_____

_____

_____

talking or speaking points _____

_____

_____

_____

key messages _____

_____

_____

_____

speculative questions _____

_____

_____

_____

leading questions _____

_____

_____

_____

loaded questions _____

_____

_____

_____

naïve questions _____

_____

_____

_____

false questions _____

_____

_____

_____

know-it-all questions _____

_____

_____

_____

accusatory questions _____

_____

_____

_____

multiple-part questions _____

_____

_____

_____

jargonistic questions _____

_____

_____

_____

chummy questions _____

_____

_____

_____

labeling questions _____

_____

_____

_____

good-bye questions _____

_____

_____

_____

reactive media relations _____

_____

_____

_____

proactive media relations _____

_____

_____

_____

EXERCISES

1. Evaluate the pre-crisis relationships at the places of business where you have worked (or where you work now). Were the pre-crisis relationships sound? Consider all types, including management–employee, management–news media, management–lawyer, and management–customer/client pre-crisis relationships.

2. When you speak about your company, do you say "We do this…" or "They do this…"? What does your response to this question say about how involved you are with your company or how important you feel you are to your company?

_____

_____

_____

_____

_____

_____

_____

_____

_____

_____

_____

_____

_____

_____

_____

_____

_____

_____

CHAPTER SIX

Case: Johnson & Johnson and the Tylenol Murders

VOCABULARY

credo _____

_____

_____

_____

product recall _____

_____

_____

_____

EXERCISES

1. *For groups:* After the tampering crisis, you are hired by Johnson & Johnson to help relaunch Tylenol in a new safety-sealed container. Research reveals that the consumer public must be "sold" on the product's safety. What would you do to "sell" the public on Tylenol?

_____

_____

_____

_____

_____

_____

_____

_____

_____

_____

_____

_____

_____

_____

_____

_____

_____

_____

_____

_____

2. Check the Johnson & Johnson Web sites—www.johnsonandjohnson.com and
    www.tylenol.com. Are there any references to the Tylenol-tampering case, which
    was never solved, or to the $100,000 reward? Are there more recent issues that
    could be prodromes to other crises? Do you see the same "open and honest" policy
    with the news media and consumer publics that existed during the crisis?

_____

_____

_____

_____

_____

_____

_____

_____

_____

_____

_____

_____

_____

_____

_____

_____

_____

_____

3. Check the Web sites of other pharmaceutical companies for information about product tampering and product failure, communication ideology, and so on. Compare and contrast what you find at the various pharmaceutical Web sites, including the Johnson & Johnson site.

_____

_____

_____

_____

_____

_____

_____

_____

_____

_____

_____

_____

_____

_____

_____

_____

_____

_____

_____

_____

CHAPTER SEVEN

Case: Exxon and the Valdez Oil Spill

CHAPTER EIGHT

Case: Exxon's Other Story—
Animal Rescue Centers and Alaskan Tourism

VOCABULARY

consortium _____

_____

_____

_____

telephone hotline _____

_____

_____

_____

EXERCISES

1. Read the following excerpts from recent articles about the Exxon crisis. How do you feel about Exxon and Captain Hazelwood after reading the excerpts? Has your attitude changed? If so, what information was most instrumental in that change? If your attitude has not changed after reading the excerpts, what other information, if any, would change it?

    a. **From Eric Nalder, "Exxon Valdez Captain: Was He Villain or Victim?" *Seattle Times*, March 14, 1999** (interview with former Valdez Captain Hazelwood).

    Ten years later, Hazelwood has never been convicted of anything more than a misdemeanor in the accident, and he still holds a valid captain's license.

    But the damage to his career has been as enduring as the damage to some of Alaska's coastline wildlife: No shipping company will risk bad publicity by hiring him.

    Hazelwood was the master of [the Exxon Valdez] in March 1989, when his third mate and his helmsman missed a simple dogleg turn and drove his 214,000-ton tanker into the shoals of history....

    There was the 10-degree turn his third officer failed to make in time—a "no brainer" so simple that some maritime schools have stopped using the accident scenario as a testing example of ship simulations. "It was a routine maneuver...."

    The 3rd officer is now 2nd mate on a U.S. flagged bulk ship....

    Both the courts and the Coast Guard rejected the most serious charge of drunkenness.... He was sentenced to 1,000 hours of community service on a misdemeanor conviction for the wrongful discharge of oil....

    Exxon later merged with Mobil, making the largest corporation on the planet....

    "Hazelwood was just a pawn," said Dan Lawn, an environmental inspector and the first Alaska state official to board the vessel after the grounding.

    Paul Larson, a retired U.S. Coast Guard commander who investigated and prosecuted Hazelwood during his license revocation hearing, said, "I spoke to people up and down the coast at different ports. Without exception, everyone I talked to indicated he was highly skilled, highly qualified. He's basically being black-balled." (pp. A1, A26)

    b. **From "Serving Time," *People*, July 12, 1999.**

    Working as hard as he has, the new guy at Bean's Café, an Anchorage soup kitchen, has made quite an impression. "He's a cut above the normal worker," says manager George Hieronymous. "The clients and staff really like him."

    [Hazelwood was] ordered to perform 1,000 hours of community service.... [A]fter spending his first day picking up trash on local roads, Hazelwood was transferred to the soup kitchen to protect him from still angry locals. (p. 62)

c. From Jayne Clark, "10 Years After the Exxon Valdez Oil Spill, a Cleaner Alaska Is Awash in Tourists," *USA Today*, **March 5, 1999.**

A decade later, the economy is on the mend and tourism is thriving. Who would have guessed an environmental disaster would be good for business?

The Sound's heightened popularity is, in part, because of an overall tourism boom in Alaska, while visits have doubled in a decade to 1.3 million annually. But the unprecedented media attention brought by the Exxon debacle broadened public awareness of this rugged slice of south-central Alaska....

"One of the positive spins of the spill is that people are much more familiar with Prince William Sound and the towns on it," says Tina Lindgren, executive director of the Alaska Visitors Association. (p. A1)

d. From Joel Connelley, "Exxon Says It Has Paid Enough for Valdez Oil Spill," *Seattle Post-Intelligencer,* **May 4, 1999.**

The Exxon Corporation mounted a multipronged legal offensive here yesterday, urging the 9th U.S. Circuit Court of Appeals to set aside the record $5 billion award to fishermen and others damaged by the 1989 Exxon Valdez oil spill....

The company claimed that it already has paid out $2.2 billion in cleanup costs, more than $1 million in civil settlements and criminal fines, [and] dispersed $300 million to fishermen and fish processors. (pp. A1, A6)

e. From "EEOC Sues Exxon Over Drug and Alcohol Policy," *Minneapolis Star Tribune*, **June 14, 1998.**

Exxon Corp. put a new policy into place that any employee with a history of drug or alcohol abuse could not work in any of 1,500 safety-sensitive jobs.

The company, eager to avoid another Valdez disaster, applied the policy to plant operators, drivers, and ships' mates after news reports surfaced that the captain of the Valdez … had been drinking and that Exxon officials knew he had sought treatment for his drinking problem four years before the accident. Hazelwood was later cleared by a jury of intoxication charges ….

The U.S. Equal Employment Opportunity Commission (EEOC) in Dallas has sued Exxon, contending the company's rule that employees in safety-sensitive jobs cannot have a history of drug or alcohol abuse violates the Americans with Disabilities Act.

"Exxon is stigmatizing people because of their previous disability records," said Jeff Bannon, regional attorney for the EEOC. (p. 5D)

2. What do you think Exxon can do now to improve its reputation?

_____

_____

_____

_____

_____

_____

_____

_____

_____

_____

_____

_____

_____

_____

_____

_____

_____

_____

_____

_____

_____

_____

_____

_____

_____

_____

3. The document shown in Fig. 8.1, "Exxon Bird and Otter Rescue Center Media Relations," summarizes the public relations campaign funded by Exxon. Soon after the *Valdez* oil spill, Exxon hired George Mason, then-vice president of Bradley/McAfee Public Relations (now Bradley/Reid Communications) in Anchorage, to head the campaign. The principal account executive was Suzanne Stolpe-Bishop. For the campaign, the agency won the prestigious Aurora Award for Excellence from the Alaskan chapter of the Public Relations Society of America (PRSA) in 1990. Read the document, and then compare it to criticisms of Exxon's public relations effort during the *Valdez* oil spill crisis.

Exxon Bird and Otter Rescue Center
Media Relations
A Public Relations Campaign

On March 24, 1989, The Exxon Valdez ran aground in Prince William Sound, well-known as a region with diverse wildlife populations, some of which are on the endangered species list. In the wake of the 11 million gallon spill, many marine mammals and birds were expected to be oiled and would therefore be in danger. Exxon acted quickly to contact the nation's leading experts in the fields of bird and sea otter rescue. Alice Berkner, R.N., of the International Bird Rescue and Research Center, and Randall Davis, Ph.D., of Seaworld Research Institute, arrived in Valdez 2 days after the spill and had facilities and teams in place 2 days later. Their first "patients" arrived the same day.

So did the national and international media corps. Bombarded by media requests and visits, Exxon contracted a spokesperson to develop media strategies and act as a liaison between the media and the centers.

OBJECTIVES:

1. To gain reasonable control of the media blitz.

2. To respond positively and quickly to media requests.

3. To convey factual information during press conferences, thereby reducing the need for journalists to go to the centers to collect information/updates.

4. To convey the positive message that everything possible was being done to care for the oiled birds and otters by Exxon and its contractors.

PLANNING:

Exxon public affairs officers and the spokesperson met to assess the situation and choose a path. The centers had been likened to a "MASH" unit, and indeed, the number of sick and dying patients kept the staff and volunteers working around the clock. Two journalists had disrupted a press conference inside the bird center by fighting and, as a result, the center had been closed to all journalists. An or-derly schedule of media tours for the more than 100 was developed. It was determined that the spokesperson would give updates at the daily Exxon press conferences and would be available 24 hours a day.

EXECUTION:

First-come, first-served media tours were conducted twice daily. The spokesperson conducted the tours, and one of the two center directors was available for a limited time for questions.

In addition, media opportunities were developed, such as: the first otter pup, the transport of the first otter pups out of state, the first bald eagle, the first bird release, the first otter release. When the animal's health required it, the media were asked to pool their resources: one videocamera and one still photographer were allowed in the area, and then the footage and photos were made available to all media representatives. Special arrangements were made for journalists who wanted to do longer feature stories—requiring them to work as volunteers in the centers for a prescribed period of time.

The daily press conferences were used to update animal/bird counts and release information. Program directors attended only when the issues required their statements.

Another key to success was simple: Only the media liaison gave statements to the press. This policy ensured consistent statements and allowed the directors the luxury of referring questions to the media liaison until it was convenient for them to meet with journalists. In the crisis situation, the policy immediately smoothed communications and freed the directors to work in the centers where they were needed.

Exxon, the "sponsor" of the centers, chose to take a back seat during the operation of the rescue centers. Exxon officials always responded when questioned, but they often referred questions about specific aspects of the program to the media liaison. Again, this ensured consistency.

RESULTS:

After initial frustration at not having carte blanche access to the centers, journalists responded very positively to the new media policies. The centers' staff members were able to treat their "patients" with little distraction, and journalists were able to get the stories they wanted without fighting the whole press corps.

The message was consistent, and Exxon was able to be shown taking positive steps in a very emotional situation, for a very emotional area of the cleanup.

The result was thorough, consistent stories about many aspects of the rescue operations, and a significant aspect of the international news coverage on the spill.

The staff also gave presentations to five tourism associations and conventions on a variety of public relations topics, and in the process further established a successful working relationship with these industry sources.

RESULTS:

We had no previous baseline to measure results against. However, our program resulted in more than half a mile of favorable newspaper column inches in the 18 months we have held the contract. This does not include magazines, television or radio, or articles generated by other Alaskan services; nor publicity generated as a direct result of our efforts to cover the oil spill tourism crisis.

Highlights of our evaluations include:

Over 2,000 press kits distributed worldwide.

We've responded to over 1,000 toll-free telephone calls for assistance from editors and writers.

Providing writer/editor assistance to more than 30 major magazines in the United States for travel stories and three television programs, one of which won an Emmy.

Providing fact-checking services for the development of two new and two rewritten travel books on Alaska.

Total newspaper column inches for the period July 1, 1988 through June 30, 1989 of 21,779 with a combined circulation of 43,039,244. This represents an equivalent advertising value of an estimated $2.2 million, and a return on investment (ROI) for our public relations budget of more than seven to one.

Of the above statistics, our penetration into the 21 A and B markets (those cities with the highest tourism responses) during the eighteen months was 47% of our effort. This resulted in 13,236 newspaper column inches in only these markets, with a combined circulation of over 51 million and an equivalent advertising value estimated at $2.1 million.

Although the final statistics are not yet compiled, early indications seem to show that tourism in Alaska in 1989 exceeded any previous year—despite the expected disastrous effects of the Valdez oil spill.

FIG. 8.1. A summary of the Exxon public relations effort after the *Valdez* oil spill.

CHAPTER NINE

Case: Snapps Restaurant and the AIDS Rumor

VOCABULARY

damage-control task force _____

_____

_____

_____

war of public opinion _____

_____

_____

_____

EXERCISES

1. What damaging rumors have you heard about companies, organizations, or individuals. Research them and try to determine their origin. If the rumors were false, how could they have been stopped or alleviated? Did you believe the rumors initially? Why or why not?

_____

_____

_____

_____

_____

_____

_____

_____

_____

_____

_____

_____

2. Design an advertisement with graphics for the Snapps free hamburger giveaway. Recall that the restaurant had the giveaway to get customers back after the teenager confessed to circulating the AIDS rumor with a crudely written flyer. Your design, however, should not be as crude as the flyer was.

CHAPTER 10

Case: Cellular Phones and the Cancer Scare

EXERCISES

1. In discussing the cellular phone crisis, Ken Woo, Cellular One's media relations manager, described a three-tier program that was aimed at the consumer public. The *first tier* gave speaking points to customer service representatives and other employees who received calls from customers:

   a. Customers and the public are being unnecessarily frightened.

   b. Cellular One sympathizes with the family involved, but the lawsuit has no merit.

   c. Scientists conclude that cellular phones are safe.

   The *second tier* included materials sent to customers: a cover letter from the company's general manager and a position paper about the safety of cellular phones. The *third tier* was used to arrange for customers to speak with key executives who could take further action.

   Now imagine that you are a Cellular One PR employee. Write a brief but convincing letter to customers about their cellular phones for use in the second tier.

   _____

   _____

   _____

_____

_____

_____

_____

_____

_____

_____

_____

_____

_____

2. Ken Woo wrote a crisis plan and guidelines for crises prior to the cellular phone crisis (see Figs. 10.1 and 10.2). Which items in his plan were crucial during the cellular phone crisis?

_____

_____

_____

_____

_____

_____

_____

_____

_____

_____

_____

_____

_____

Managing the Crisis
By Ken Woo

ADVANCE WARNING

1. Move to disclose risks, problems, and soon immediately to defuse any kind of speculative story that could cause undue harm.

2. When time permits, it is often beneficial to coordinate a press disclosure of an event with interested government officials. A joint statement could preclude their "jumping on the bandwagon" against Cellular One.

3. Notification of employees in advance of public disclosure is important whenever possible. Such notification replaces rumor.

DURING A CRISIS

1. Take charge. Manage the situation. Control coverage.

   • Limit media access to premises

   • Limit media access to employees

   • Designated spokesperson is the only person to make a statement to insure clarity and consistency

2. Access facts. Develop a fact sheet. *Who, what, why, when, where,* and *how.* Whenever possible, communicate facts to employees first before public release.

3. Measure the emotional response.

4. Determine the risks to consumers/customers/employees.

5. Define and prioritize actions necessary to protect those at risk; rank and prioritize options and resources.

6. Communicate the risks and company actions undertaken to protect people from those risks.

7. Move and communicate decisively.

8. Eliminate the risks/causes of crisis in the minds of those exposed to them.

9. Think long-term to preclude reoccurrence.

FIG. 10.1. Cellular One's brief crisis plan written by Ken Woo, media relations manager. (*Source*: Printed with permission of Ken Woo.)

> **Ken Woo's**
> **Communications Guidelines**
>
> 1. Lasting perceptions are set in the first 24–48 hours. Our communications policy is to provide factual, timely information.
>
> 2. Consumers are first concerned with how we will protect their ability to access the systems against actual disaster risks. To be successful, we must quickly demonstrate actions to protect the public, including all disclosure of any threats or risks.
>
> 3. When it comes to health, safety and products, people are not rational. Facts generally don't dominate perceptions. Emotions and emotional symbols do.
>
> 4. Trust can only be built through effective communications of our commitment to contain and control potential risk.
>
> 5. Zero risk is a myth and the publics know it. They want options and controls. They can't make a risk-benefit judgment if they are not adequately aware of options and controls. We must inform.
>
> 6. In communicating about health and safety aspects of products, recognize in advance what communications will be memorable and persuasive to people.
>
> 7. Communications without concern are apt to fall on deaf ears. Recognize and acknowledge that people can be concerned about and afraid of product risks.
>
> 8. Identify, cultivate, and hold onto third-party allied supporters in the community, industry, media, etc. They are essential to ongoing communications crisis matters.

FIG. 10.2. Ken Woo developed these crisis communications guidelines for Cellular One. (*Source:* Printed with permission of Ken Woo.)

DISCUSSION AND ACTIVITIES

1. Note the following quotes—positive and negative—about the possible dangers of cellular phone use. Jot down your thoughts about the quotes in preparation for class discussion.

Positive Quotes

a. From *Microwave Journal,* May 1997.

A recent National Research Council report may help put to rest the longstanding controversy about possible health risks from weak power frequency (60Hz) electromagnetic fields. The report, an exhaustive and critical review of the scientific literature dating back to before World War II up to the present, found no persuasive evidence for cancer or other chronic illness often attributed to such fields. Expert committees have searched the literature repeatedly and have found no credible evidence.

b. From *Communications Daily,* May 23, 1997.

A study in Finland at the Finnish Centre for Radiation and Nuclear Safety reveals that tests using mice to assess cancer development concluded that radio waves did not promote illness, although some research is needed before final conclusions are made. The study exposed 19 people and mice to radio waves emitted by phones and found "it was clear" that the brain converts signals into heat, but levels were well below hazardous levels.

c. From the *Baltimore Sun,* March 27, 2000.

Critics [of cellular phone research] say that just because something happens in a test tube doesn't mean the same thing will happen in the human body.... Even if it turns out cell phones do not cause cancer, cell phone users won't necessarily live long healthy lives. One thing nearly everybody agrees on: cell-phone users who gab and drive are far more likely to die in a car accident.

Negative Quotes

d. From the Associated Press, May 10, 1997.

An 18-month mouse study shows that mice exposed to radio signals similar to those produced by cellular phones were twice as likely to develop cancer as their unexposed counterparts. The study does not come close to showing that cellular phones are hazardous, but it does raise questions that need to be investigated before the devices can be declared completely safe.

e. From *Mobile Phone News*, January 12, 1998.

   The latest issue of the *Medical Journal* in Australia reports that Dr. Andrew Davidson believes the country's cancer registry data—showing that from 1982 to 1992 the incidence of brain tumors at a hospital in Western Australia increased 50 percent for men and 62 percent for women—is due to the use of cellular phones.

f. From *Seattle Times*, December 14, 1999.

   "Rats exposed to microwave radiation similar to that emitted by cell phones suffered long-term memory loss," says Henry Lai, a bioengineering research professor at the University of Washington. Lai advises, "Don't avoid cell phones and don't linger on them worry free." Users are advised to keep calls to five minutes and use headsets for longer conversations.

g. From *Seattle Times*, May 16, 1996.

   Cellular phones can dangerously interfere with the operation of heart pacemakers when they are very close to the electronic heart stimulators, it was reported by researchers of the North American Society of Pacing and Electrophysiology, specialists in cardiac-rhythm disorders.

h. From *The Daily Mail*, July 16, 1998.

   Scientist David Cogill, campaigning for warning labels on mobile phones, said, "Anyone who uses a mobile phone for more than 20 minutes at a time needs to have their head examined."

_____

_____

_____

_____

_____

_____

_____

_____

_____

_____

_____

_____

_____

_____

Case: United Way of America and the Overspending CEO

Case: United Way of King County and the Overspending CEO

VOCABULARY

United Way of America _____

_____

_____

_____

local United Way organizations _____

_____

_____

_____

satellite teleconference _____

_____

_____

_____

pro bono public relations counsel _____

_____

_____

_____

editorial board _____

_____

_____

_____

PR Newswire _____

_____

_____

_____

EXERCISES

1. In developing a list of lessons learned during the United Way of America crisis, former PR director for United Way, Sunshine J. Overkamp, was intentionally general in her phrasing of each lesson (see Fig. 11.1). What more specific lessons might she have learned from the United Way crisis to help the PR department avoid a similar crisis in the future?

_____

_____

_____

_____

_____

_____

_____

_____

_____

_____

_____

_____

_____

_____

_____

_____

_____

_____

_____

_____

_____

_____

_____

Sunshine J. Overkamp's Lessons Learned

1. Communicate your positive message day-in and day-out before any crisis hits. People will not listen to you …in the middle of or directly following a crisis. Invest now in positive, day-to-day communications.

2. Rumors are worse than reality. Follow up on and investigate all rumors, while remembering that not all are based on facts.

3. It is not enough for just the communications staff to be ready for a crisis. Other staff and boards must be prepared also.

4. All constituencies count. Make sure you have a list of all your constituencies now. Otherwise, during a crisis someone will be overlooked. Don't forget your internal constituencies—they are extremely important.

5. There is a huge difference between good and bad reporters. Spend your time with the good ones.

6. It is extremely important to involve all the people who can help you during a crisis. A good lawyer who understands the importance of the court of public opinion can be one of your best allies.

FIG. 11.1. Sunshine J. Overkamp, former United Way PR director, listed these general lessons learned from the United Way crisis involving the overspending of William Aramony. (*Source*: Printed with permission of Sunshine J. Overkamp).

2. Assume that you are a PR professional for United Way of King County. Write a letter to a donor who is concerned about the agency's connection to Aramony.

CHAPTER THIRTEEN

Case: They Keep Coming—
Chinese Immigrants in Canada

VOCABULARY

Canadian Charter of Rights and Freedoms _____

_____

_____

_____

Canadian Immigration Act _____

_____

_____

_____

Canada's Privacy Act _____

_____

_____

_____

refugee status _____

_____

_____

_____

China's one-child rule _____

_____

_____

_____

onn-governmental organization (NGO) _____

_____

_____

_____

NIMBY _____

_____

_____

_____

Canadian government ministers _____

_____

_____

_____

Figures 13.1, 13.2, 13.3, 13.4, 13.5 are political cartoons which appeared in Canadian newspapers during the crisis. Your instructor may use them in assignments. You should understand their significance to the issue.

FIG. 13.1. This political cartoon was published in the *Vancouver Province* on July 26, 1999. (*Source*: Reprinted by permission of the *Vancouver Province.*)

FIG. 13.2. This political cartoon was published in *The Glove and Mail* on September 14, 1999. (*Source*: Reprinted with permission from *The Globe and Mail*.)

FIG. 13.3. This political cartoon was published in the *Ottawa Citizen* on September 4, 1999. (*Source*: Reprinted by permission of Syndicam Productions.)

FIG. 3.4. This political cartoon was published in the *National Post* on January 5, 2000. (*Source*: Reprinted with permission from the *National Post* and the artist, Gary Clement.)

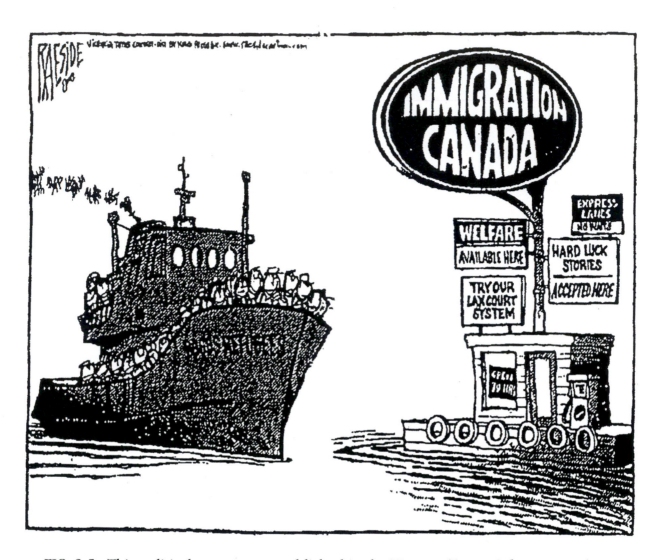

FIG. 3.5. This political cartoon was published in the *Victoria Times-Colonist* on July 22, 1999. (*Source*: Reprinted with permission from the artist, Adrian Raeside.)

CHAPTER FOURTEEN

Case: DC Mayor Anthony Williams
and Another "N" Word

VOCABULARY

niggardly _____

_____

_____

_____

ghost employees _____

_____

_____

_____

Wall Street bond rating _____

_____

_____

_____

below-investment-grade rating _____

_____

_____

_____

near-investment-grade rating _____

_____

_____

_____

media stakeout _____

_____

_____

_____

CFO _____

_____

_____

_____

EXERCISES

1. Check back issues of local and national newspapers to see if they covered the crisis. Did local people (in your area) make remarks about the issue? Compare the newspaper coverage in large and small cities, in big cities with large black populations (e.g., Detroit, Atlanta, and Philadelphia), and in cities with small black populations (e.g., Seattle, Portland, and Salt Lake City).

_____

_____

_____

_____

_____

_____

_____

_____

_____

_____

_____

_____

2. City employees were not mentioned in the crisis communications. How would you, as spokesperson, communicate with employees? What would you say? Write your message or statement to employees.

_____

_____

_____

_____

_____

_____

_____

_____

_____

_____

_____

CHAPTER FIFTEEN

Case: Texas A&M University and the Bonfire Tragedy

VOCABULARY

Bonfire tradition _____

_____

_____

_____

"Aggie Spirit" _____

_____

_____

_____

timeline _____

_____

_____

_____

Critical Incidence Response Team _____

_____

_____

_____

mock press conference _____

_____

_____

_____

EXERCISES

1. Cynthia Lawson, in a previous job, was part of a mock crisis. If she were to plan a mock crisis at Texas A&M, how could it work? Who would be the players? What information would it reveal? How could it help the university prevent or cope with future crises?

_____

_____

_____

_____

_____

_____

_____

_____

_____

_____

_____

_____

2. Imagine that it is only a few days after the bonfire accident. Parents of deceased and injured students have been notified. Write a letter to parents of students not injured in the bonfire tragedy. Although these parents already know their children were not harmed, they need some reassurances.

_____

_____

_____

_____

_____

_____

_____

_____

_____

_____

_____

_____

3. Check the Texas A&M University Web site (www.tamu.edu) for information on the bonfire and other traditions. Jot down the pros and cons of these traditions in preparation for class discussion.

_____

_____

_____

_____

_____

_____

_____

_____

_____

_____

_____

_____

4. Read the news release "Texas A&M President Postpones Bonfire for 2 Years," shown in Fig. 15.1. Which publics does the decision satisfy? In addition to safety precautions, what reasons might explain the university's decision to temporarily suspend the bonfire tradition?

Texas A&M President Postpones Bonfire For 2 Years

COLLEGE STATION - Texas A&M University will suspend its traditional bonfire for two years, President Ray M. Bowen announced Friday during a news conference.

Bowen said the postponement of the bonfire until 2002 at the earliest was necessary because restructuring the design and planning construction of the event could not be properly done until that time.

"If the restructuring I have described is successfully completed, we will have a bonfire in 2002," Bowen said. "If that construction is judged successful by the certification process, then we will have a 2003 construction.

"You can expect important memorials and other events to occur in 2000 and 2001. The details of these events will need to be developed by our students," Bowen added.

On Nov. 18, 1999, the bonfire stack collapsed, killing 12 Aggies and injuring 27 others.

Bowen said significant changes will be required to ensure safe future bonfires. Among the changes he outlined were:

• A single tier "teepee" design.

• A bonfire construction plan prepared by licensed professionals.

• Construction time limited to two weeks, with no work performed after midnight.

• All logs will be cut by professionals and delivered to the construction site.

- The construction site will be a fenced-in area with limited access and monitored by video cameras.

Bowen said he will begin working with students, faculty, and staff to begin the planning of the 2002 bonfire, with their finalized plans due by April 2001.

He said his decision on the bonfire is not the defining event for the future of Texas A&M. "Our character as an academic institution of exceptional quality and our character as an academic institution that produces leaders are not dependent on the decision I announce today," he explained.

"The character of Texas A&M flows from the Aggie Spirit. This spirit is a manifestation of our academic strength, a manifestation of the character of the people of A&M, and [a] manifestation of our history and those uncountable intangibles that make Aggies special.

"My bonfire decision places great responsibility upon our student leadership," Bowen said.

"It requires that they work with us to meet the conditions I have described. In doing so, they will be committing to fundamental changes in all aspects of the bonfire, changes which none of them would ever have anticipated before last Nov. 18. They will be required to commit to processes which protect not only the students [who] build the 2002 bonfire, but the students [who] will build all future bonfires.

"It will be their responsibility to implement the cultural change necessary to see that the horror of the bonfire collapse never visits our campus again."

Bowen said his decisions regarding the bonfire were not made in haste.

"I understand and respect the interest in this decision on the part of members of the A&M community," he said. "Our history and our traditions are important to all of us. The bonfire is one of the major traditions. It is not the defining activity of the university. It is one of many manifestations of what we call the 'Aggie Spirit.' If somehow we did not have a bonfire, the Aggie Spirit would manifest itself in another beneficial activity just as it does in so many others at Texas A&M. The special character of this university and its people is not, in my opinion, defined by any one tradition."

Bowen added, "I have heard from people who say this decision rivals the most difficult decisions that have been made throughout our history. People equate it with the decision to admit women and the decision to make the Corps of Cadets optional. I think that I am uniquely qualified to tell you that these assessments are wrong.

"Frankly, the bold decisions which were made in the mid- to late-1960s to commit Texas A&M to nationally prominent academic programs were more important to A&M than any decision on the bonfire."

Bowen said all of his decision were based on "one simple truth: I do what is best for the university and its students. Regarding the advice I have received from the Aggie community, it is easy to summarize. A small number of people have advised me that the bonfire should be ended, a small number have said the bonfire should continue with minimum changes.

"The remainder, a vast number of people, have advised [me] to continue the bonfire only if it can be made a safe student activity. This large group advocates making whatever changes are necessary in order to have a safe bonfire."

He added, "It is my decision that this restructuring must produce a well-managed bonfire student project which is forever safe, which projects a positive image for the university and which does not place detrimental time demands on students."

FIG. 15.1. This June 6, 2000 news release announced plans to suspend the Texas A&M bonfire tradition until at least 2002. (*Source*: Texas A&M University *Aggie Daily* Web site: http://www.tamu.edu/aggiedaily/press/. Reprinted by permission of Texas A&M Office of University Relations.)

5. Imagine that you are a spokesperson for Texas A&M University at the time of the crisis and that a news service from another state or country wants to run photos of students on your campus after it hears about the bonfire tragedy. Examine the four photos shown in Fig. 15.2. Select the one photo that best says, "Our students are concerned about each other." Mark the photos you do not want to use because they say, "The university is a dangerous place." Would you allow the news service to use the photo of the female student with the cigarette in her hand? Why or why not?

_____

_____

_____

_____

_____

_____

_____

_____

_____

_____

_____

_____

_____

_____

_____

_____

_____

_____

_____

_____

_____

FIG. 15.2. These four posed photos depict scenes of students reacting to word that several students on their campus were killed in a bonfire accident. (They are meant for discussion of photos only and in no way are intended as actual depictions of Texas A&M students in grief.) (*Source*: Used by permission of K. Fearn-Banks, Inessa Freylichman, and Justin Schutz.)

CHAPTER SIXTEEN

Case: U.S. Postal Service and Workplace Violence

VOCABULARY

news availability _____

_____

_____

_____

news conference _____

_____

_____

_____

Employee Assistance Program (EAP) _____

_____

_____

_____

EXERCISES

1. Check the U.S. Postal Service Web site (www.usps.com) for data on workplace vio-
    lence. What do you find?

    _____

    _____

    _____

    _____

    _____

    _____

    _____

    _____

    _____

    _____

    _____

    _____

    _____

    _____

    _____

    _____

    _____

    _____

    _____

    _____

    _____

    _____

    _____

    _____

    _____

2. Examine Table 16.1 and determine, in your state, which category of occupational fatality is of most concern. How would you devise an employee relations and communications program to help reduce this type of fatal injury? What would be the key messages? What experts would you consult and possibly quote? Compare the table data for your state with the data for other states. Are the statistics higher or lower, considering population?

_____

_____

_____

_____

_____

_____

_____

_____

_____

_____

_____

_____

_____

_____

_____

_____

_____

_____

_____

_____

_____

_____

TABLE 16.1
Fatal Occupational Injuries by State and Event or Exposure, 1998

State of Injury	Total Fatalities[a]		Event or Exposure[b] (% of state total for 1998)				Exposure to harmful substances or environments	
	1997 (revised)	1998	Transportation incidents[c]	Assaults and violent acts[d]	Contact with objects and equipment	Falls		Fires and explosions
Total[e]	6,238	6,026	44	16	16	12	9	3
Alabama	139	135	49	13	16	5	13	3
Alaska	51	43	70	16	–	9	–	–
Arizona	61	71	41	13	18	10	13	6
Arkansas	102	86	48	10	17	12	8	5
California	651	617	40	24	11	13	9	1
Colorado	120	77	49	12	19	12	5	–
Connecticut	32	55	35	19	5	16	13	–
Delaware	17	11	45	–	–	–	–	–
District of Columbia	23	13	–	48	23	–	–	–
Florida	366	384	42	22	9	15	11	2
Georgia	242	195	41	17	16	15	8	3
Hawaii	19	12	58	–	–	25	–	–
Idaho	56	51	53	6	20	8	10	–
Illinois	240	216	37	18	17	16	11	2
Indiana	190	154	53	18	12	9	7	–
Iowa	80	68	50	–	21	13	9	4
Kansas	93	98	53	8	12	3	12	11

continued on next patge

| | Total Fatalities[a] | | Event or Exposure[b] (% of state total for 1998) | | | | | |
State of Injury	1997 (revised)	1998	Transportation incidents[c]	Assaults and violent acts[d]	Contact with objects and equipment	Falls	Exposure to harmful substances or environments	Fires and explosions
Kentucky	143	117	38	14	27	12	9	–
Louisiana	137	159	45	13	13	7	12	11
Maine	19	26	50	–	23	15	–	–
Maryland	82	78	50	21	6	9	10	4
Massachusetts	69	44	34	9	20	20	11	–
Michigan	174	179	30	18	20	12	12	8
Minnesota	72	84	40	4	32	11	10	4
Mississippi	104	113	50	14	13	9	9	4
Missouri	123	145	53	12	17	14	10	3
Montana	56	58	50	22	7	14	5	–
Nebraska	46	56	59	9	20	–	9	–
Nevada	55	60	50	25	7	12	–	7
New Hampshire	23	23	43	22	17	13	–	–
New Jersey	101	103	43	14	19	14	8	3
New Mexico	50	48	40	15	15	6	12	10
New York (including N.Y.C.)	264	243	32	22	15	17	8	6
New York City	109	94	11	41	12	20	6	10
North Carolina	210	228	49	16	17	11	7	–
North Dakota	35	24	42	–	46	–	–	–

Ohio	46	186	201	11	18	13	5	6
Oklahoma	49	75	104	9	17	9	11	–
Oregon	54	72	84	8	24	7	7	–
Pennsylvania	43	235	259	15	18	9	10	6
Rhode Island	50	12	11	–	–	–	–	–
South Carolina	42	110	131	22	14	11	10	–
South Dakota	54	28	23	–	32	–	–	–
Tennessee	49	450	468	12	17	7	15	–
Texas	41	523	459	15	15	11	14	4
Utah	57	67	66	–	12	15	9	4
Vermont	38	16	9	–	25	–	–	19
Virginia	43	176	166	23	15	13	6	–
Washington	44	112	112	9	14	12	13	7
West Virginia	33	57	53	7	39	12	–	5
Wisconsin	51	97	114	18	20	6	5	–
Wyoming	73	33	29	–	9	–	9	–

[a]Includes other events and exposures, such as bodily reaction, in addition to those shown separately.
[b]Based on the 1992 BLS Occupational Injury and Illness Classification Structure.
[c]Includes highway, nonhighway, air, water, and rail fatalities and fatalities to workers struck by vehicles.
[d]Includes violence by persons, self-inflicted injuries, and assaults by animals.
[e]Includes fatalities that occurred outside the territorial boundaries of the 50 states.

Note. Percentages may not add to 100 because of rounding. Dashes indicate less than 0.5% of data that are not available or that do not meet publication criteria. *Census of Fatal Occupational Injuries,* 1997–98.

Source: Bureau of Labor Statistics, U.S. Department of Labor, in cooperation with state and federal agencies.

3. Read the new story, "Shooting Tragedy Rocks UWMC," in Fig. 16.1. Then consider the prodromes in the following list and answer these questions: Which were the most significant prodromes for the hospital shooting? Which could have been heeded to avoid the crisis? Which showed a naive outlook on the part of hospital administrators? What could the hospital administrators do now to avoid similar incidents in the future? How can the UW Medical Center personnel be protected? How can a public relations program help in this prevention?

   a. Before the shooting, the would-be assailant's computer was found open to an Internet map of local gun shops.

   b. Days later, he bought a gun and then told a police officer and university officials that he did so "because America is a dangerous place." He was told of a law against guns on campus. However the law is not enforceable until someone uses or shows a gun, which is often too late.

   c. He made no threats to anyone. His e-mail messages to supervisors at first asked for another chance; then later they became more despondent and angry. One e-mail said, "I am totally lost." There was more concern that he would harm himself than others. But some residents locked their office doors at the sight of him.

   d. Lacking an imminent threat, authorities said they could not do more than offer counseling for his emotional turmoil and tutoring to improve his English skills. Administrators feared repercussions if they were to order a psychological evaluation because he might consider the order demeaning and offensive.

   e. The murder–suicide was termed "unique" and "unprecedented." No one had ever responded to failure in that way at UWMC.

   f. The assailant was a hard-working employee who, officials said, "was not as good as he wanted to be." He was slow and made mistakes, such as placing specimens in unlabeled jars. When corrected, he responded, "But I know what's in there."

   g. He was a naturalized American, but his basic culture was Chinese. The following questions arose after the incident: If he was a failure, how could he face his family in China? Would he be shamed? Chinese culture has different ideas about psychological health and different traditions of suicide.

   h. Administrators decided it would be impractical to post a police officer in the area to screen the thousands of hospital employees for weapons.

   _____

   _____

   _____

   _____

   _____

Shooting tragedy rocks UWMC

By Jason Sykes
Daily Staff

Tomorrow the friends, co-workers and family of Dr. Rodger Haggitt will gather in the Health Sciences Building's Hogness Auditorium to honor a life dedicated to increasing knowledge and understanding.

It appears no one will ever be able to explain his death, however.

Haggitt was a victim of a murder-suicide perpetrated last Wednesday by Dr. Jian Chen, a resident whose one-year stint with the UW was about to come to an end. Colleagues said Chen looked upon Haggitt as a "father figure," making the events of that afternoon even more difficult to comprehend.

Chen stopped by his mentor's office as planned around 3:30 p.m. for a meeting, most likely to discuss his future after leaving the UW pathology program. The 42-year-old resident had known for six months that his UW contract would not be renewed but had not yet landed another residency elsewhere despite concerted efforts by Haggitt and others.

At about 3:45 p.m., witnesses heard yelling followed by a series of shots. When [the] police entered the room, both men were dead—Haggitt of four gunshots to the body and Chen of a self-inflicted wound to the head.

A series of notes discovered by police in the course of their investigation confirmed that Chen did intend to commit suicide, but they did not suggest he planned to harm Haggitt. And although university officials were alarmed when they discovered Chan's plan to purchase a firearm, he assured both them and the police that he only wanted it for personal protection.

"He said America was a dangerous place," said Dr. John Gienapp, the director of graduate medical education program assessment and development. He added that Chen never threatened anyone at the UW before last week's shooting, although several of his coworkers were worried he might try to harm himself.

Chen came to the UW's prestigious program—which he referred to as his "golden opportunity"—after a year's residency at the University of Mississippi. Previous to that, he'd studied in Texas, Iowa, and New York as well as in his native China.

But almost from the onset of his residency, Chen struggled with the grueling work load and academic demands of the curriculum. His problems were compounded, former advisors said, by his difficulties with the English language.

Dr. Nelson Fausto, the chair of the school's pathology department, said Chen was repeatedly encouraged to seek tutoring to improve his communication skills but doubts that he ever took advantage of the options offered to him.

By November the decision was made to terminate Chen's contract "in the best interest of all parties involved," according to Fausto. Chen was informed of the decision and offered both career and psychological counseling; however, he seemed indifferent to the former and flat-out refused the latter. As far as anyone at the UW could tell, Chen hadn't made any progress in his search for a new position before his death, even though most residents typically secure a place in a program by late March.

Still, Fausto said, no one could ever have predicted last Wednesday's tragedy.

"Looking back, I don't think we would do anything differently," he said.

Dr. Eric Larson agreed, and although the UWMC will review the case thoroughly to see if it warrants any future upgrades in security, the early prognosis is that nothing drastic would change.

"This is a single incident—the med school has been open 40 years and nothing like this has ever happened be-fore," Larson said, adding that it wasn't "practical" to screen all of the center's visitors for guns. The sprawling south campus complex of classrooms, libraries, laboratories, and a working hospital sees an estimated 55,000 people pass through it each day.

For 15 years one of those people was Haggitt, age 57, who arrived at the UW in 1985 as an already established pathologist. Not content to rely on his reputation, Haggitt consistently pushed the research envelope in his specialty, gastrointestinal pathology, winning several prestigious awards and even serving as president of the Gastrointestinal Pathology Society.

He also was a respected mentor in the UW's pathology program.

"The residents intensely enjoyed working with him," said Fausto, who added that the program could never replace Haggitt.

FIG. 16.1 News story of UW Medical Center murder–suicide in the *Summer Daily*, July 5, 2000. (*Source*: Used with permission of the *Summer Daily* of the University of Washington).

4. Write a news release based on the 1993 statement made by then-Postmaster Marvin Runyon in Fig. 16.2. Your news release should be written for newspapers that did not attend the press conference at which Runyon delivered the statement.

STATEMENT BY MARVIN RUNYON
PRESS CONFERENCE ON THE SHOOTINGS
IN DEARBORN, MICHIGAN, AND DANA POINT, CALIFORNIA

Dearborn, Michigan
May 7, 1993

When a crisis strikes, it's important to respond with compassion and action. We have taken steps to do both in the past 24 hours.

Since the tragedies of yesterday, our first concern has been the well-being of our employees and their families. We have visited our injured employees in the hospital, talked with family members, and are working to provide the special support they need during the is difficult time.

In Dearborn, crisis professionals were on site within the first two hours yesterday. Employees have received counseling and the opportunity to discuss their feelings. About a dozen employees with severe emotional reactions have been referred to Oakwood Community Hospital. We are continuing to provide counseling today. We have taken the same actions in California. And, at all of our locations that have experienced a crisis situation over the last several years, local managers are setting up seminars and counseling for the employees.

Violence in the workplace is unacceptable in any form. This includes harassment, verbal or physical intimidation and, of course, the senseless killings of yesterday. In the past several months, we have taken steps to deal with these problems in the Postal Service.

We have strengthened our hiring practices. We have expanded training in our personnel function and improved screening procedures. We have made our people aware of the types of military discharges that are indicative of problems. And we are working to get more complete information on criminal records and military histories on possible employees.

Postal management and labor have also taken joint actions to remove the root causes of hostility from our workplace. We have a task force that meets monthly and is working on [the] detection, prevention, and response to violence in the workplace. We have established a crisis hotline telephone number for all employees, staffed 24 hours a day at Headquarters. This number has been communicated throughout the system.

With input from an all-employee opinion survey completed last year, we have begun measuring management performance in 20 categories, and they have been incorporated into our goal of setting a performance appraisal processes. Today, promotions and one-third of management compensation are tied to their people skills.

Now, we must do more.

Within the week, all of our districts across the country will set up focus groups with employees of all levels and local counseling professionals. We will discuss the recent crises, possible problems, and actions employees want us to take to safeguard the work site.

Our district and plant managers will now have the authority to acquire local counseling services and to take the actions they consider necessary to protect the security of their employees. We also will provide local hotline numbers, monitored by professionals, so employees can communicate outside their normal chain of command.

That leaves us with one final issue. How can we deal with employees who are identified as potentially violent but who have taken no actions on which management or the authorities can act?

The facts are these. We can identify some of these employees through their behavior with managers, supervisors and coworkers. We can refer them to the Postal Inspection Service for interviews and, in some cases, for professional psychiatric evaluation.

However, the presence of a psychiatric disorder or the potential for violence is not cause for disciplinary action against the employee. Unless the individual is found by the psychiatric professional to be specifically dangerous or takes some inappropriate or even extreme action, neither we or other authorities can act. The problem that we face in these instances is the same one faced by our free society in general.

As I said yesterday, we are deeply concerned and frustrated that, in spite of our efforts to prevent violence, senseless tragedy has happened within the ranks of the Postal Service. We are committed to doing everything within our power to prevent and eliminate any violent behavior within the Postal Service in the future.

Finally, I want to thank the postal employees, local crisis support people, and the communities of Dearborn and Dana Point for the outpouring of concern and sympathy they have extended to us, to the victims, and to their families. Their compassion is appreciated as we begin the long recovery from these incidents.

Thank you. That concludes my statement. I will take your questions.

FIG. 16.2. The transcript of a 1993 statement by then-USPS Postmaster Marvin Runyon following two incidents of violence at postal facilities that year.
(*Source*: Printed with permission of Roy Betts, U.S. Postal Service.)

CHAPTER SEVENTEEN

Case: The Metro Transit Accident: Driver Shot, Bus Flies Off the Bridge

VOCABULARY

police radio scanner _____

_____

_____

_____

soft news _____

_____

_____

_____

media relations ideology _____

_____

_____

_____

banner headline _____

_____

_____

_____

5-column photo _____

_____

_____

_____

anniversary story _____

_____

_____

_____

EXERCISES

1. Search the Metro Transit Web site (http://transit.metrokc.gov) for information about measures that have been put in place in response to the 1998 tragedy or other prevention efforts. Also look for later incidents that may be prodromes. What do you find?

_____

_____

_____

_____

_____

_____

_____

_____

_____

_____

_____

2. Read Fig. 17.1. Your instructor may assign a writing project based on it.

_____

_____

_____

_____

_____

_____

_____

_____

_____

_____

_____

_____

_____

JOINT STATEMENT ON TRANSIT SECURITY
Metro Transit and ATU Local 587
November 30, 1998

The weekend's event was highly unusual and not typical of transit security incidents. Nevertheless, it brought us together today to help us focus on a serious issue.

We came out of this meeting with an organizational commitment to improving the safety and security of our system.

We are also agreed on the need for improved communication and cooperation between union and management on this issue.

In the next two months, we will look at our current security services and take the following actions:

- pull our base security committees together to meet individually and then together in a workshop to help identify issues and potential strategies

- explore the issue of physical protection for drivers, including barriers or enclosures

- explore the issue of technology; we are currently testing video camera systems and we will develop a recommendation on that technology

- evaluate what other systems are doing to protect drivers in this country and around the world

- evaluate officer deployment strategies and explore alternatives

Finally, we have agreed to continue meeting together weekly to monitor our progress and to stay on top of this issue.

FIG. 17.1. The joint statement issued on November 30, 1998, by Metro Transit management and the local union of bus drivers. (*Source:* Printed with permission of Dan Williams)

3. There were 11 bus routes overall with assaults in the first 11 months of 1998. These routes also had the most passengers. The assaults ranged from fare disputes and evasions to the 1998 shooting. Planning a campaign to communicate with riders on various routes is an example of segmenting publics (see chap. 1).

_____

_____

_____

_____

_____

_____

_____

_____

_____

_____

_____

_____

_____

_____

_____

_____

_____

_____

_____

_____

_____

_____

4. Read the op-ed piece shown in Fig. 17.2, written by Rick Walsh, the general manager of Metro Transit, a month after the tragedy. Is the article convincing as far as safety on Metro buses is concerned? What is its primary intention—to convince passengers to continue riding the buses, to get new riders, to show Metro's concern about safety, or to express the agency's corporate point of view? Why doesn't the article indicate what future measures will be taken?

_____

_____

_____

_____

_____

_____

_____

_____

_____

_____

_____

_____

_____

_____

_____

_____

_____

_____

_____

_____

_____

The Management: Making a Secure System Safer
By Rick Walsh

This community suffered an enormous loss Nov. 27 when one man's actions caused Metro Transit's Route 359 bus to plunge off the Aurora Bridge. We will never be the same.

To say the least, this has been a difficult time for us at Metro. We have had to face the loss of a longtime employee. We have had to deal with the fact that the lives of 32 valued customers have changed forever, and that the life of one of them has ended. We have had to contend with an overwhelming news media, as reporters and editors probe for answers and try to make sense out of a senseless act.

And we have had to face the fact that many of our bus drivers, the backbone of our system, are frightened, angry and tired of the abuse they can experience as they simply try to do their jobs.

In the wake of last month's tragedy, three distinct questions about Metro's transit security program have emerged. Is Metro indifferent to the safety and security of its drivers and customers? Is the transit system unusually dangerous and growing worse? Is transit security different or separate from broader public safety issues?

One thing needs to be made clear: Nobody in this community should think for one second that the safety of our drivers and passengers is unimportant to Metro, or that we lacked a strong security program before Nov. 27. Here are the basic elements of our transit security program:

- A $5 million transit security budget in 1998, a 50 percent increase since 1995.

- Special transit police unit created this year, with a King County Sheriff's Office captain and five sergeants managing and supervising a force of off-duty Seattle Police Department officers and King County sheriff's deputies.

- Eight more full-time deputies included in the 1999 budget have already been added to special transit police unit.

- About 45 officers and deputies deployed each day to police the transit system in cars, on bicycles, at transit facilities and riding buses.

- Direct phone lines from Metro radio personnel to local police jurisdictions throughout King County to summon police to bus incidents.

- Automatic vehicle location and an emergency alarm system for drivers.

- Public Safety Partnership Program, with volunteer bus drivers attending community meetings, visiting schools and staffing community events to talk to people about what they can do to report or stem unruly behavior on Metro buses.

- Customer Code of Conduct posted in buses, providing the legal framework to eject unruly customers from buses, or arrest them, or in some cases ban them from the system entirely.

These enforcement measures and community programs are making a difference. We have a substantially safer system now than we did 10 to 12 years ago. As measured by statistics kept by the Federal Transit Administration, our system compares favorably with many cities of similar size or with comparable transit systems. Even one assault is too many. But consider the fact that our buses travel 40 million miles, are in service for 4 million hours and record about 100 million passenger boardings a year.

Day in and day out, no one has more contact with and exposure to the public than bus drivers.

Transit security should not be viewed in isolation. What happens on our buses is a reflection of the communities in which they operate. Buses in the Aurora Avenue North corridor, for example, are vulnerable to the same public safety problems common to that area. And our exposure is great in that area. We're not there just once in a while. We operate more than 745 trips every week up and down Arurora Avenue North between downtown Seattle and Shoreline, providing service almost around the clock, from 5 a.m. until 2 a.m. Policing that service is a challenge not only for us, but also for the Seattle and Shoreline police departments.

The Seattle area has grown and changed over the past 20 years. That growth has brought with it the problems and issues that face any large metropolitan area. The great majority of people who live here value the comfortable environment that has been called "Northwest nice." Unfortunately, some either can't or won't live up to that standard of behavior.

Is our system dangerous? By most measures, no. But there is no doubt that disruptive passengers can create an uncomfortable and intimidating environment on a bus. Nobody with any sense of decency wants that kind of climate to prevail on our transit system.

The best way—the only way—to deal with transit security issues is to confront them head on. We repeat now what we have already made clear to our employees: This organization is committed to working with our employees, our riders and local police departments to improve the safety and security of our system.

Rick Walsh is general manager of King County Metro Transit.

FIG. 17.2. An op-ed piece written by the general manager of Metro Transit and published in a local newspaper. (*Source*: Printed with permission of Metro Transit.)

5. An excerpt from a *Seattle Post-Intelligencer* news story published nearly a year after the bus tragedy is reprinted in Fig. 17.3. What questions might a reporter ask to complete the story? What information would probably be included in the rest of the story? Which questions would be aimed at the Metro Transit spokesperson? Which questions would be asked of other persons? Why isn't the bus driver's name mentioned in the story? Do you think it was the reporter's decision alone or was she influenced by Metro Transit?

Metro Driver Attacked by Woman With Knife

A routine morning commute ended in bloodshed yesterday when a veteran Metro Transit bus driver was stabbed by a passenger wielding a paring knife and ranting about demons and sunspots.

The woman, who was later arrested, attacked the 53-year-old driver before 9 a.m. as he ferried passengers from downtown Seattle to Queen Anne Hill.

As the bus turned into Broad Street from Third Avenue, the unruly rider stood and shouted, distracting the driver and other passengers.

"The passenger was creating a disturbance and annoying the other passengers, but the driver didn't have any sense that she was dangerous," said Metro spokesman Dan Williams.

When the driver warned her to sit down or get off, the woman screamed: "I'll kill you and I'll drive the bus myself!" Then she lunged at the driver.

As he struggled to control the moving bus, stunned passengers watched the woman jab a 3-inch knife into the driver's left hand....

FIG. 17.3. An excerpt from a news story written by Kimberly A. C. Wilson for the *Seattle Post-Intelligencer* on November 19, 1999, one year after the 1998 Metro bus shooting and accident that left the bus driver, the assailant, and a passenger dead.

6. According to Table 17.1, Metro Transit bus, routes 7 and 174 were the most dangerous to drivers and passengers in 1998. Other than through news media coverage,
   how could Metro Transit persuade riders of routes 7 and 174 that it has improved
   bus safety? Should Metro Transit plan a communications program for passengers
   riding routes 307 and 42? Why or why not?

TABLE 17.1

Number of Assaults on Metro Transit Buses During an 11-Month Period in 1998 (*injury and noninjury assaults*)[1]

	Against Drivers			Against Passengers		
Route	Injury Assaults	Noninjury Assaults	Total Driver Assaults	Injury Assaults	Noninjury Assaults	Total Passenger Assaults
7	1	6	7	4	22	26
174	2	3	5	8	19	27
6	3	2	5	3	12	15
359[2]	1	3	4	0	2	2
36	1	3	4	2	7	9
150	2	2	4	1	6	7
106	0	4	4	0	7	7
21	0	2	2	4	1	5
42	0	0	0	0	2	2
307	0	2	2	0	1	1
48	0	3	3	0	4	4

[1]Some "noninjury assaults" included refusals to pay fares.
[2]Express version of route 6.
Source: King County Metro Transit, 1998.

Case: Alpac Corporation and the Original Syringe-in-the-Can Scare

Case: Pepsi and the National Syringe-in-the-Can Crisis Scare

VOCABULARY

news satellite _____

_____

_____

_____

hoax _____

_____

_____

_____

market share _____

_____

_____

_____

EXERCISE

1. Read "What Pepsi Did Right" (Fig. 19.1) and "Working With the Media" (Fig. 19.2), both written by Pepsi headquarters personnel, and answer the following questions:

    1. Do the tactics in both articles apply to the work of the agency in Washington state?

    2. Number 5 of "Working With the Media" is "Choose the right spokesperson." Who were the spokespersons for the Alpac crisis? The national crisis?

    3. Number 6 is "Use formats reporters use." Examine formats of reporters and columnists in your local newspapers.

Working With the Media

One advantage Pepsi had going into the syringe hoax was the company's broad experience working with the media on everything from the new advertising and marketing efforts to financial and environmental issues.

A half-dozen PR managers worked daily with reporters and editors. There are seven tactics they used throughout the syringe case.

1. **Assess the problem through the public's eyes.**
   Take responsibility for getting the facts in a clear, reasonable way.
   Demonstrate that trust in you is well-placed.

2. **Speak with one voice.**
   Don't comment off the cuff. Be certain there is a single, unified voice.
   State the facts when you know them and be definitive.

3. **Communicate quickly.**
   Be quick, be fresh, and provide information as soon as it's available.
   When the issue is resolved, tell the public it's over.

4. **Keep your message simple.**
   Too many facts can be overwhelming, especially when crammed into TV sound bites.
   Also, think visually. Show as well as tell. Video is one of the top news-making tools today.

5. **Choose the right spokesperson.**
   Pepsi president Craig Weatherup considered addressing the public during the syringe crisis "part of my job" even though he had never received formal media training. During a crisis, consumers want to see where the buck stops.

6. **Use formats reporters use. Distribute media-friendly tools.**
   Make spokespersons accessible to the media round the clock because news happens in real time. It interrupts programs or lands as a teaser for the 11 p.m. news. Use tools media can use: video, diagrams, photos. If you give the media tools they can use, you stand a much better chance of getting your message out than if you just issue a statement and let them fill in the blanks.

7. **Present the people, not the company.**
   Nobody loves a company. They love products and people. The more you can personalize and involve people, the better. "We concentrated on what consumers care about ... the can of Pepsi in their hand, not some kind of assault on Pepsi's national name," crisis coordinator Rebecca Madeira said. "We also gave them as many opportunities as we could to see real people solving real problems."

FIG. 19.1.   Pepsi headquarters developed this list of advice for working with the media after its syringe-in-the-can crisis.

What Pepsi Did Right

While there is no fail-safe formula for resolving a crisis, Pepsi's crisis management team reflected on tactics that helped them to weather the hoax:

1. Consumer safety comes first. The FDA is a strong advocate for public health—but one that can only act on the basis of the facts. "Our job was to get them the facts they needed as quickly as possible," said Pepsi's product safety expert Jim Stanley. Their job was to cover every base to make sure that the issue was being thoroughly investigated and that the public interest was being protected.

2. An open-door policy was operative from day one. "We had a unique opportunity to talk to our consumers—through the media," said Pepsi CEO Craig Weatherup. "We believed, that when presented with the facts, the American public would recognize the truth and their trust in our products would be restored."

3. Communicate fast and communicate often. Work with the media using the tools and timetables that work best for them. "The hoax story was so visual, videotape news releases distributed by satellite were the key to getting our message out," said crisis coordinator Rebecca Madeira.

4. Gain alignment with those inside and outside the company who are working on the problem. "You can't make bold decisions alone," explained Stanley. Independent, third-party counsel is critical in making judgments impacting public health and safety.

5. Speak with one voice. Input on crisis strategies comes from many camps ... each with valid but often conflicting agendas. Ultimately, consensus is key. A divided camp erodes confidence, disrupts the process, and breeds skepticism.

6. Clearly define the roles of each and every person on the crisis team and practice working together. The Pepsi team and its suppliers were "road tested" on smaller issues. During the crisis, the team followed the same process ... only at warp speed.

7. Informed employees, especially those on the front lines, make a tremendous difference in getting our message out. Keep them updated on what's happening and why. Give them the tools to pass important messages along to our customers, quickly and easily.

8. Feedback is essential. It's important to gauge how well your message is getting across. Use survey instruments like overnight telephone polls, consumer calls to an 800 number, sales data, customer input, and employee feedback to evaluate the effectiveness of the plan. Make course corrections as necessary.

9. Benchmark. The time to build your crisis plan is not during a crisis. Benchmark great companies. Learn from them. Stay up to date on tools, technologies, and services that can be enlisted on-the-spot to help out in a crunch.

10. Know thyself. Use your mission statement as your conscience; it will help guide your actions. Pepsi's operating philosophy is a commitment to put customer needs and concerns ahead of our own. This approach was an invaluable "reality check" and helped us to define the crisis issues in their eyes rather than our own.

11. Take every consumer complaint seriously. Never question the integrity of any individual. Let the authorities investigate and render judgment.

FIG. 19.2.   These are the strategies and tactics that Pepsi feels made the company emerge from the crisis successfully.

Case: California State University, Northridge, and the 1994 Los Angeles Earthquake

Case: Southern California Gas Company and the 1994 Lost Angeles Earthquake

VOCABULARY

Natural disaster _____

_____

_____

_____

Photographic icon _____

_____

_____

_____

Telephone tree _____

_____

_____

_____

EXERCISES

1. Consider the expression, "Luck is limited." How could you relate this expression to CSUN's efforts during the crisis?

_____

_____

_____

_____

_____

_____

_____

_____

_____

_____

_____

_____

2. Write a 20-second PSA for CSUN based on the information in the news release, "Special Information for Cal State Northridge Community," shown in Fig. 20.1. Twenty seconds is about 50 words, so you cannot use all of the news release information in your PSA.

_____

_____

_____

_____

_____

_____

_____

_____

_____

_____

_____

CALIFORNIA STATE UNIVERSITY, NORTHRIDGE
Contact: Bruce Erickson
Kaine Thompson

PRESS RELEASE

SPECIAL INFORMATION FOR

CAL STATE NORTHRIDGE COMMUNITY

NORTHRIDGE-January 23, 1994 - Due to the Northridge Quake, the Cal State Northridge campus has been officially closed until all buildings can be evaluated and certified as structurally sound. Until this is accomplished, the Cal State Northridge community is advised of the following:

- Faculty and staff will be notified by phone or mail when to report to work.

- Registration (TTR) and classes have been postponed.

- Campus officials anticipate that Spring Semester will begin February 14.

- Intersession classes postponed. Arrangements for completion will be announced when Spring Semester begins.

- Please do not come to campus until you have been notified.

- Call 818-XXX-XXXX, beginning Friday, January 28, for a pre-recorded message for the latest information.

FIG. 20.1. A CSUN news release following the 1994 earthquake. (*Source*: Printed with permission of Cal State Northridge's University Relations Dept.)

3. Could the news release in Fig. 20.1 have been written prior to the earthquake, with
    blanks for specific information? If so, why? If not, what kind of news release could
    have been prepared in advance of an earthquake?

_____

_____

_____

_____

_____

_____

_____

_____

_____

_____

_____

_____

_____

_____

_____

_____

_____

_____

_____

_____

_____

_____

_____

4. Write a news release for the *Los Angeles Times* based on the information Fig. 21.1, "The Gas Company Employee Earthquake Relief Fund," an announcement made to employees of the Southern California Gas Company in 1994. Your news release should be dated February 1, 1994.

_____

_____

_____

_____

_____

_____

_____

_____

_____

_____

_____

_____

_____

_____

_____

_____

_____

_____

_____

_____

_____

_____

_____

_____

THE GAS COMPANY EMPLOYEE EARTHQUAKE RELIEF FUND

Gas Company employees needing earthquake relief assistance can apply for a grant from the <u>G</u>as Company <u>E</u>mployee <u>E</u>arthquake <u>R</u>elief (GEER) Fund.

Grants are available up to $500 for qualified applicants who need assistance with:

- Food
- Shelter
- Transportation
- Other emergency necessities

Applications are available in each region and headquarters facility. This is not a loan, and your ability to repay is not a factor. The GEER Fund is provided through employee and Company donations. Multiple grants may be available, depending upon need and availability of funds. Part-time employees with more than one year of service and all active, regular employees are eligible to apply.

The Geer Fund needs your support!!! If you want to help other employees who need assistance, please send your check, payable to "GEER Fund, c/o CCF," to Carolyn Williams, ML 25FO.

The GEER Fund is established through the California Community Foundation, and is administered by a Gas Company employee review committee.

For more information, please call.

"GEER" UP TO HELP OUR EMPLOYEES

FIG. 21.1. Southern California Gas Company's announcement to employees about a special grant program set up for them after the 1994 earthquake. (*Source*: Printed with permission of Chance Williams, S.C. Gas Co.)

5. Note that Southern California Gas Company prepared two radio PSAs—one in English (Fig. 21.2) and the other in Spanish (Fig. 21.3) for release on the same day. Because Los Angeles has a very large Hispanic population, the PSA to Spanish language radio stations was a necessity. Considering the changing demographics of the United States, what does this tell you about the future of public relations strategies and tactics?

```
RADIO

Client:     The Gas Company              Date: 1/24/94          Job#: 137-477

Title:      Earthquake Recovery Message  Length: 60             Code: SCGS 0580

Revision: Version 2, Rev. 1              Face: 1
```

LIVE ANNCR:

In the aftermath of the earthquake, The Gas Company would like to let our customers know the following: your safety is our first priority. Next is resuming service as quickly as possible. We have over thirty-four hundred workers and volunteers from neighboring utilities in the field. The bulk of the work will be completed this week. To help us help all customers, we're asking that you refrain from making non emergency service requests. For safety reasons, homes and businesses that sustained major damage will not have gas service turned back on until the premises have been declared safe. We're also asking customers to check for signs of appliances shifting, vents separating, or signs of damage to walls near gas appliances which could indicate an unsafe condition. If any of these conditions are found, shut off gas to the individual appliance and call a licensed heating-plumbing contractor or The Gas Company at 1-800-XXX-XXXX. And please remember that we will need access to the premises to restore services.

FIG. 21.2. The English version of a 1994 Southern California Gas Company PSA. (*Source*: Printed with permission of Chance Williams, S.C. Gas Co.)

CLIENT: The Gas Company   SCRIPT TITLE: Service Disruption

PRODUCT: Earthquake   TRACK #:

JOB #: 94-SCG-   AIR DATE:: ASAP

LENGTH: :60   MEDIA: Radio

DATE: 1/24/94   REV: 01

LIVE:

Este es un mensaje importants de la Compania de Gas.

A consecuencia del terremoto, en The Gas Company queremoe hacerle saber que, muestra primera prioridad es su seguridad, y luego, restaurar el servicio lo antes possible.

Tenemos una fuerza laboral de 3,400 empleados que van de casa en para restaurar el servicio. Esperamos que la mayor parte del servicio sea restaurado esta semana.

Para que ayudemos a todos los clients, pedimos que se abstenga de hacer llamadas de servicio que no sea de emergencia.

Por rezones de seguridad, no podremos restaurar el servicio de gas donde haya habido dafios serlos hasta que se haga una final inspeccion que declare su hogar libre de peligro. Inspeccione sus aparatos de gas para ver si nota dafios o cambios de posicion. Cheque si se han dafiado las salidas de aire de la calefaccion o las paredes cerca de sus aparatos de gas. Si Usted sospecha de algun problema, corte el gas al aparato y llame a la Compania de Gas o a un professional certificado de calefaccion o plomeria.

Recuerde tambien que necesitaremos acceso a su hogar para restaurar los servicios. Y durante este periodo de recuperacion, llame solamente para servicio de emergencia al 1-800-427-2200. Pida que le atiendan en espanol. Es el 1-800-427-2200.

FIG. 21.3. The Spanish version of the 1994 Southern California Gas Company PSA shown in Fig. 21.2. (*Source*: Printed with permission of Chance Williams, S.C. Gas Co.)

CHAPTER TWENTY-TWO

Useful Web Sites

NEWSPAPER SITES

Atlanta Journal & Constitution: http://www.accessatlanta.com
Boston Globe: http://www.boston.com/globe
Boston Herald: http://www.bostonherald.com
Chicago Sun-Times: http://www.suntimes.com
Chicago Tribune: http://www.chicagotribune.com
Christian Science-Monitor: http://www.csmonitor.com
Common Denominator: http://www.thecommondenominator.com
Dallas News: http://www.dallasnews.com
Dallas Times: http://www.dallastimes.com
Globe and Mail: http://www.globeandmail.com
Houston Chronicle: http://www.chron.com
Los Angeles Times: http://www.latimes.com
Miami Herald: http://www.herald.com
New York Daily News: http://www.nydailynews.com
New York Post: http://www.newyorkpost.com
New York Times: http://www.nytimes.com
Seattle Post-Intelligencer: http://www.seattlep-i.nwsource.com
Seattle Times: http://www.seattletimes.nwsource.com
USA Today: http://www.usatoday.com

Wall Street Journal: http://www.wsj.com
Washington Post: http://www.washingtonpost.com
Washington Times: http://www.washtimes.com

TELEVISION NETWORK AND NEWSMAGAZINE SITES

ABC-TV: http://www.abc.com
CBS-TV: http://www.cbs.com
NBC-TV: http://www.nbc.com
CNN: http://www.cnn.com
"Dateline NBC": http://www.msnbc.com/news/DATELINE-Front.asp
"60 Minutes": http://www.cbsnews.cbs.com/now/section/0,1636,3415-412,000.shtml
"20/20": http://www.abcnews.go.com/onair/2020/2020Index.html

GOVERNMENT AND LEGAL SITES

Equal Employment Opportunity Commission (EEOC; includes definitions of harassment and discrimination; instructions on everything form employee records to the Americans with Disabilities Act): http://www.eeoc.gov

BUSINESS SITES

Hovers Online: (profiles more than 50,000 companies) http://www.hoovers.com
InterNIC (search for domain names of companies running competing sites: http://www.internic.net
U.S. Occupational Safety and Health Administration (OSHA; provides guidelines for preventing and dealing with workplace violence, illness, and injury): http://www.osha.com
WSB-TV Atlanta (includes video interviews of business professionals and information on various types of business, including public relations): http://www.wsbtv.com
Yes Webcast Channel (includes interviews with the founders of Yahoo!, Enterprise Rent-a-Car, Birkenstock, and other successful entrepreneurs): http://www.sayyes.com

MEDIA AND PUBLIC RELATIONS SITES

CEO Express (includes links to numerous daily, weekly, and monthly online publications): http://www.ceoexpress.com
Internet News Bureau (writes news releases for companies, suggests which journalists should get them, and sends them electronically): http://www.newsbureau.com
Idea Site for Business (includes free access to more than 1,800 e-mail addresses of reporters): http://www.ideasiteforbusiness.com

Infobeat (delivers personalized daily news by e-mail): http://www.infobeat.com

Public Relations Society of America (PRSA): http://www.prsa.com

WorkinPR.com (Jobsite with supplementary information on the PR information industry, PRSA, and Council of Public Relations firms): http://www.workinpr.com

ACADEMIC RESEARCH IN PUBLIC RELATIONS SITE

PR Bibliography Books for Graduate Research: http://www.lamar.colostate.edu/~hallahan /hbibgrad.htm

RUMOR SITE

Urban legends: urbanlegends.miningco.com. Annotated updated list of Internet hoaxes and e-mail rumors.